PRS Public Relations System (BO) · Photo/Art Barut

SABIEM ESPRIT

We are changing the concept of elevator

Through the Esprit project, Sabiem and **GIUGIARO** DESIGN disclose the future of elevators.
The soft elliptical lines of mirror and car instrumentation, the rounded design of walls, the countless number of pastel nuances for the "liquid-fabric" painting, all of them lend to the new elevator a character that looks soft and feels original to the touch.
The comfort, safety and technology of Sabiem elevators have found their new shape in the balanced and beautiful project by **GIUGIARO** DESIGN

Sabiem Esprit heralds the evolution of the concept of elevator

In Groningen art prepares for eternity. With Meg.

The Museum of Modern Art in Groningen, designed by Alessandro Mendini, is a work of art in itself, as any visitor perceives as soon as he crosses its threshold. What's more, the masterpieces arrayed on its walls can count on additional protection on their voyage into eternity: the protection of Meg. Meg stands up to the test of time and fights off any attacks from wind and weather without threatening the natural environment. Used with great success for many years, especially abroad, Meg comes with the guarantee of Abet Laminati experience. It does not contain asbestos or other polluting substances. Meg combines optimum protection with the ability to reduce air pollution. Available in a range of 36 colours, Meg represents the leading edge treatment for buildings and urban fixtures. Major architects like Vittorio Gregotti and Alessandro Mendini have employed Meg on important projects that bear witness not just to the resistance but also the aesthetic qualities of Meg which is a Print HPL product.

For further information on our products fill in this coupon and send it to: Abet Laminati SpA, Viale Industria 21, 12042 Bra (CN), tel. 0172/419111, fax 0172/419524.

Name_______________________________________

Telephone___________________________________

Adress______________________________________

Company____________________________________

ABET LAMINATI

Meg. The revolution in exterior paint.

Harry, designed by Antonio Citterio. The design idea is based on the concept of a small system, one which can be arranged so as to create seating groups that are able to meet specific functional needs. The system is made up of sofas that come in

three different lengths and by sectional pieces, including right and left end pieces, a
middle piece, a corner piece and chaise longue end piece. The "double depth" seating
is the main feature of all these pieces, which can also be lined with a loose cover.

Castelli SpA
Azienda certificata ISO 9001 o UNI-EN 29001
Via Olmatello, 21 - 40064 Ozzano dell'Emilia (BO)
ITALIA - Tel. 051/6513711 - Fax 051/6513799

3D

L'UNICO

SISTEMA

PER

UFFICI...

VERAMENTE

APERTI

CASTELLI®

Arredamenti per l'ufficio e la collettività

Molteni & C.   20034 Giussano   Telefono: Telex: Telefax:
Via Rossini 50 (Milano) Italia   (0362) 851334 330188   (0362) 354448
Luca Meda
Piroscafo

Molteni&C

La pubblicazione di questa rivista
è possibile
grazie al sostegno economico
e organizzativo delle aziende:

The publication of this magazine
is possible
with the sponsorship of the
following firms:

La publication de cette revue
est possible grâce au soutien
économique et à la capacité
d'organisation des entreprises:

Ermöglicht wird die
Veröffentlichung
dieser Zeitschrift
dank der finanziellen und
organisatorischen Unterstützung
der Firmen:

Abet Laminati
B&B Italia
Castelli
Molteni & C.
Sabiem

Unless otherwise specified, all the illustrations are taken from the archives of the London Transport Museum.

Henry C Beck, first card folder edition of the London Underground Diagram, January 1933.

66 Rassegna

(London Underground)

Rassegna
Themes in Architecture

Editor
Vittorio Gregotti

Editorial Staff
Pierluigi Cerri
Dario Matteoni
Livia Piperno

Editorial Coordinator
Maresin Cavagna

Art Director
Pierluigi Cerri

Production
Maurizio Zanuso

Translations
Language Consulting
Sebastiano Brandolini
Cioni Carpi
Livia Ferrari

Collaborator
Francesca Molteni

**This issue edited
by Sebastiano Brandolini**

Quarterly
year XVIII, 66 - 1996/II
Publisher: CIPIA srl/Editrice Compositori srl
via Stalingrado 97/2, 40128 Bologna, Italy
tel. (51) 32.79.29, 32.78.11, fax (51) 32.78.77
Editorial Offices: via Matteo Bandello 20
20123 Milano, Italy, tel. (2) 481.41.41-481.24.48
fax (2) 481.41.43-481.24.48
Rassegna
© copyright 1996
CIPIA srl
Registered in Milan, Italy
Price: Lire 45,000
Back issues: Lire 49,000
Subscription: one year (4 issues) Lire 156,000
Subscriptions: CIPIA,
via Stalingrado 97/2, 40128 Bologna, Italy
tel. (51) 32.79.29, fax (51) 32.78.77
Distribution worldwide:
Birkhäuser-Verlag für Architektur,
Klosterberg 23, P.O.Box 133, CH-4010 Basel,
tel. (41-61) 205.07.07, fax (41-61) 205.07.92
Advertising representative:
Editrice Compositori srl,
via Stalingrado 97/2, 40128 Bologna, Italy
tel. (51) 32.78.11, fax (51) 32.78.77
Color by Graphicolor srl, Milano
Printed by Tipografia Compositori srl, Bologna

*This issue was produced thanks to the collaboration
of the London Transport Museum, especially of Sam
Mullins, Director, and Sheila Taylor, Senior Assistant
Curator, whose readiness to co-operate never failed.*

4

Introduction

Over the years London and its Underground have developed a powerful association, almost a reciprocal identity. The Underground map has become a symbol, reproduced on major consumer items as though it were a work of abstract art; meanwhile, to operate properly, the traffic of Central London depends more than ever on the well-being of its underground circulation system, where you can breathe the civic awareness and sense of unity of the capital, even though it remains difficult to find the money to combat its visible deterioration.

The Underground is to be found in literature and at the cinema, it is a place of artistic and musical expression, a tourist attraction. From the standpoint of transport, it is the urban extension of the radial railway lines whose terminals join up around the centre. This hybrid nature is important if we are to appreciate the fascination it exercises compared with the undergrounds of Paris, New York, Berlin, and which can be discerned in the carriages, the walkways, the timetables, the tunnels, the open-air sections. Indeed that is why the Underground has recently become a monument of transport archaeology. By the residents and the tourists who crowd London, the Underground is seen less and less as a "service pure and simple," but as something more, and in any case as unique and different. The Underground too has its own history and memory, and a beauty of its own, and for this reason it has become an object to be conserved. Many think that it was a precursor of modernity, but if it becomes an object of worship, it will no longer live as a modern object. This is one of the many dilemmas that London Transport must face in the near future, whether it remains a public company or is privatized.

We live in a period in history in which every architectonic construction can change the way it is used, in a certain sense it can separate from its origins, and also from the surrounding world. Today the Underground can also decide to be something else, compared with the way it was imagined. Is it still a system – a "tube" – just like so many other tubes that lie under the ground in London? Perhaps it has become a space that effectively synthesizes the lifestyle of our century? Or perhaps it should be considered as a root grown underground from a plant whose shoots are outside enjoying the sunlight? Several of the articles collected here try to answer these questions, and investigate the relations between the city and its entrails. The fact remains that the beginning and end of the Underground are difficult to establish, and its bounds have become more and more imprecise as it has gradually grown.

Over the years the relations between the city and its bowels have become intricate, stratified and complex to manage, and are running the risk of causing embolisms on the tracks, on the platforms, in the tunnels, at the barriers. For engineers the Underground is a flux made up of just numbers of people and dimensions in centimetres, a conduit where the laws of physics for liquids apply. For architects, however, it is a huge public space, with hierarchies and ramifications, decorations and commercial spaces, a sort of hidden network with the same attributes as the streets on the surface. The two perceptions, of the engineers and the architects, meet and clash at the intersections. Almost every station in the centre is an intersection. The intersections are the genetic code of the system, points of transit and stopping, much sought-after commercial spaces; today they are treated as architectural categories in their own right.

Yet it is not only in the heart of the capital that the Underground makes the city; in the 1930s the Underground encouraged significant growth of the suburbs, making them plausible in financial and design terms; and the map distorted their distance so as to make them appear much closer to the centre than they actually were. Alongside the Underground there arose civic centres, shops and cinemas, small monuments of classicist language. To date the Underground has enjoyed a great unity of language, and this has made each line particular and the system recognizable as something organic. Today's administrators would no longer have the courage or the chance to support a project so complex and composite, to bring it to a conclusion: today's democracy envisages diversified commissions and pluralist ideas.

After the Victoria Line of the 1960s – which indicated a positivist optimism in the industrial design and a cool image – today the extension to the Jubilee Line is being built, in the East End astride the Thames, from Westminster to Canary Wharf and beyond. This artery will save Canary Wharf from certain failure in financial and design terms, since in any case the roads would be inadequate to support the traffic. The Jubilee Line will have an image of its own only along the tracks; on the surface and in the connections each architect has invented his own *underground* language, inevitably conflicting with the idea of public "service" that was once referred to. In this game of parts, something important is lost.

Sebastiano Brandolini

1. Sewermen going to work
in the sewers, 1900 ca.
Guildhall Library, London.

2. M Brunel, *Thames Tunnel*, 1843.
Section of shaft and tunnel during
construction.

6

1

1. Sewermen going to work
in the sewers, 1900 ca.
Guildhall Library, London.

Underground London

The Underground railway system is only the most obvious aspect of London's dependence on its underground infrastructure. For many people, especially visitors to London, the London Underground provides the clearest way of understanding the city. The clarity of the Underground map and the corporate Underground graphics are in contrast to the chaos of the streets above ground.

Travellers come up to the surface, finish whatever they have to do, and then retreat underground again to rejoin a world which seems more logical and intelligible than their ground level existence.

The London Underground evokes strong feelings of loyalty (or of despair when it goes wrong) because so many people use it regularly. Indeed, for most people it provides the only time when they go deep beneath the city. Other underground services, on which London is

just as dependent, attract nothing of the same kind of interest or affection, because they are seldom seen at first hand. Like urban dwellers everywhere, Londoners turn on the light, run a bath or cook the supper without giving a second thought about how the services they are using reach their home or workplace. Even when the street is dug up to reveal the service ducts and pipes, most people, if they show any interest, cannot identify the different services and cannot say where they came from. Because for most of the time the services are buried and out of sight, they are given hardly any thought.

What is not properly realised is that the services infrastructure of London has shaped the city just as much as the Underground railways have done. Like the railways, the story is one of trying to keep abreast and ahead of urban growth and of Londoners' changing liv-

ing standards. And just as the railways have been able to deliver commuters to their work from increasingly distant suburbs, the services infrastructure has been extended till it has become an integrated part of a national network. But as anyone who travels on the Underground knows only too well, there comes a point where the number of people wanting to travel produces such acute congestion that the system no longer works: people can't get onto the trains or even onto the platforms.

Similarly, the rest of the urban infrastructure can become so congested that it threatens the amenity of the city which it is meant to serve. Streets are constantly dug up to insert new services or repair existing ones, and the ground beneath the street becomes clogged with the remains of man-made structures. The arteries which sustain the urban body begin to ossify to the point where ei-

3. Bathing in the Fleet. Engraving.
From: A. Pope, *Dunciad*, 1728.
Guildhall Library, London.

4. Fleet Ditch at Holborn Bridge,
undated drawing.
Guildhall Library, London.

8

3

4

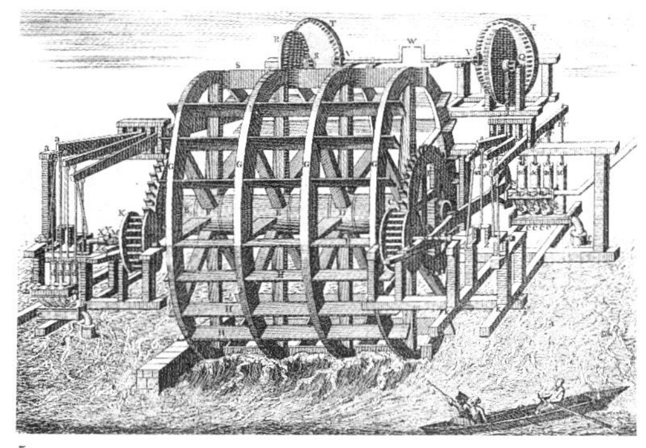

5. London Bridge Waterworks, as rebuilt by George Sorocold in 1701-2. The water-wheel, incorporated in the structure of the bridge, pumped water from the Thames for supply to buildings in the City. Guildhall Library, London.

6. Wooden water pipes of the New River Company, 1800 ca. By courtesy of the Trustees of Sir John Soane's Museum, London.

ther bypass surgery is needed or the city gradually loses its vitality.

What follows is a discussion of the underground services which deliver London its water, light, power and communications and which help dispose of London's waste. The overall historic pattern is of services that once were delivered above ground through the streets being one by one put underground in cables, pipes and ducts, and of their being delivered from further and further away. As well as the benefits of health and convenience, in theory this has improved the way streets function. It has made it easier to move about the city, because the streets are no longer congested by the fetching and carrying of basic necessities. But in practice, even when services are buried beneath the streets, they still exert a powerful influence on urban amenity and environment.

The first of London's services to be put underground was for the supply and disposal of water. The River Thames dominates London's geography, but now that it is used more as a visual amenity than as a working river it is easy to forget how crucial it is to the life of the city. Most of London's water has always come from the Thames, and for most of its history the river has also been used as a drain for waste water and sewage; a combination of functions with vicious consequences for the health of Londoners.[1] On a smaller scale, the rivers and streams which flow into the Thames have played the same dual role, with similar results for the morbidity of local districts. The Thames is still there for everyone to see, but almost all of the tributaries have now been covered over or diverted into pipes, to be remembered chiefly in the street names of the places where once they flowed; Walbrook in the City, Brook

Street in Mayfair, at least ten streets associated with the River Westbourne, and many more. Some minor rivers have never been caught and piped, but remain as surprises for the discovery of those trying to build along their course.

Concern about the pollution of the Thames and its tributaries spurred the search, from the Middle Ages onwards, for alternative sources of pure water, especially springs and wells. In 1245 the mercantile heart of the City began to be supplied with water through lead pipes from a source near Oxford Street. Subsequently, springs at Paddington were tapped for use by the City, and by the early 17th century there were sixteen supply points where City residents could get their water.[2] However, demand was sufficient to justify a far more ambitious project, the equivalent for London of the aqueducts which supply Rome

10 from the springs of the Campagna. The New River, completed in 1613 by a private company, brought water by canal from 40 miles outside London to reservoirs on the edge of the urban area: from there it was piped to customers in the City and Westminster.

Other private companies that were set up to compete were not so ambitious, but took their water from the Thames. Having been pumped into a tower, it could then flow by gravity to the households that were connected to the system. Foreign visitors to London were impressed by the copious and varied sources of supply.[3]

Water from the New River and other companies was delivered to houses through wooden pipes beneath the street pavements, the final connection into the house being made of lead. The pipes needed to be replaced every three or four years, which by having them under the pavements could be done without disrupting the traffic. The assumption, then as now, was that the amenity of people in foot counted for far less than the need to keep vehicles moving.

When water began to be piped under pressure, wooden pipes had to be replaced by cast iron ones, and after 1817 cast iron pipes were compulsory.

The advent of improved, pressurised water supplies had dire consequences for the disposal of waste water and sewage. With pressurised water, householders were encouraged to install lavatories which discharged directly into the sewers. Essentially this meant that the rivers, including the Thames, which served as London's principal sewers, became more polluted than ever; an effect made even worse by the phenomenal population growth of the early 19th century.[4]

Though the direct connection between contaminated water and infectious diseases (especially typhoid, diarrhoea, dysentery and cholera) was only gradually understood, the crisis in the condition of the Thames was obvious to every eye and nose. The solution was to prevent sewage and waste water from ever discharging into the Thames.

The main drainage system that was built 1859-65 to the designs of the Metropolitan Board of Works' engineer, Sir Joseph Bazalgette, was the most important project London had yet seen for the improvement of the City through the construction of underground infrastructure. Though opposed at first, partly on grounds of cost, the heroic scale of the project, plus its evidently beneficent aim, caught the public imagination as no similar

7

8. Covering the reservoir in Claremont
Square, Clerkenwell in 1856.
Guildhall Library, London.

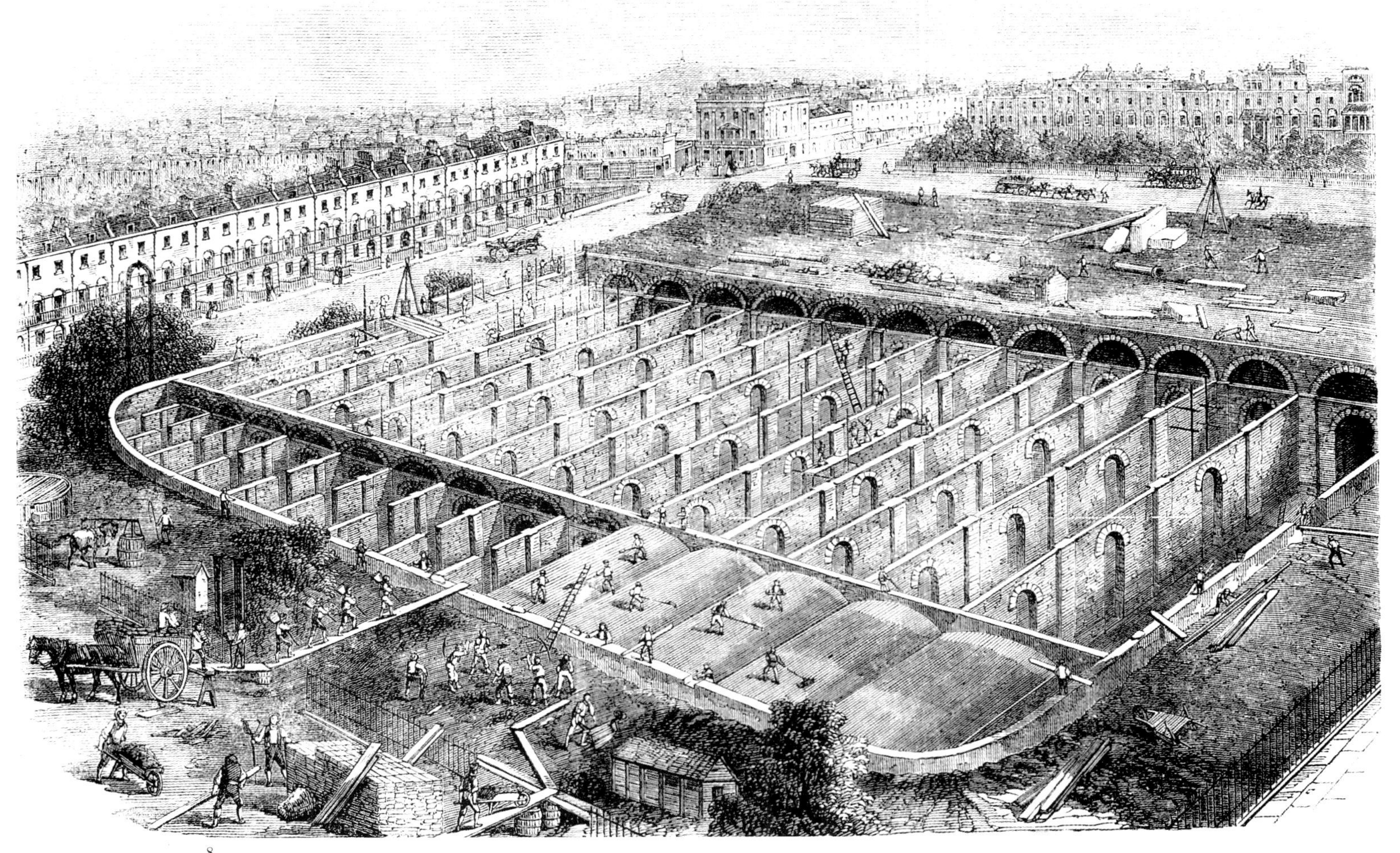

8

12

9

10

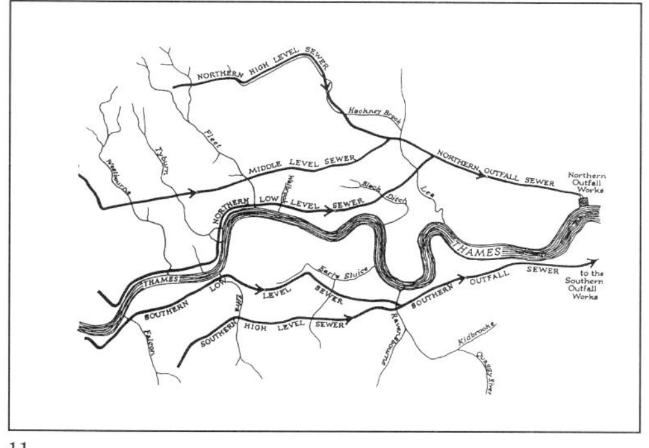

11

9. Proposal by William Capon
for embanking the Thames, 1777.
This drawing of his proposal made
in 1817 shows streets on two levels.
The houses drain directly into
the Thames.
Guildhall Library, London.

10. The Thames Embankment,
a photograph of 1885 ca.
Guildhall Library, London.

11. Sir Joseph Bazalgette's plan
for intercepting sewers, 1858. Most
of this sewer system was completed
1859-65.

12. The Thames Embankment
at Charing Cross, 1867. Engraving.
The Embankment incorporated both
Bazalgette's low level sewer and the
Metropolitan Railway (now the District
and Circle Lines). The Pneumatic
Railway beneath the Thames, shown
at the bottom of the engraving,
was never built.
Guildhall Library, London.

project has ever done. Eighty-two miles of new sewer were built, essentially as three branches running beneath the built-up area on either side of the Thames, designed to intercept the existing sewers at right-angles and divert their contents eastwards. The sewage was taken to two points 14 miles downstream of London Bridge, where it could be discharged into the Thames on the outgoing tide. One of the northern branches of the system was built as an integral part of a scheme for embanking the Thames, and survives today as the only major example in London of a project combining new infrastructure, a new thoroughfare and an underground railway.[5]

London still depends on this mid-19th century drainage system, augmented by additional sewers built in 1899-1919. And for the supply of water, the reliance on the Thames is as true today as it has ever been. The signifi-cant differences are that water is taken from the Thames further upstream, is more thoroughly purified than it ever was in the past, and is delivered via a newly completed Ring Main, which encircles London like a subterranean ring road.

In a typical London street at the beginning of the 19th century, water was the only service piped underground – the supply pipes under the pavement or the edge of the roadway, and the sewer beneath the centre of the street. Other services were delivered along the street by horse and cart – coal for heating (discharged into vaults through openings in the pavement) and oil for lighting. The delivery of heat, light and power by piped connection started in 1810, when gas production began. The immediate benefit of gas was that streets were better lit (most major London streets were gas lit by 1840), but the penalty was that each private gas company had the right to dig up the street to lay gas pipes. In places, this involved duplicate systems and thus twice the disruption. By 1850, 2,000 miles of cast iron gas main had been laid, supplying gas from small scale, local gasworks.[6] Houses had begun to be lit by gas, but it was not until a system of metered prepayment had been invented in 1888 that gas cooking and heating were widely adopted.

The gradual amalgamation of small private gas companies encouraged the development of much larger capacity gas works, necessitating much larger mains to distribute gas to wider areas. With the advent of natural gas (first discovered under the North Sea in 1959) all of these gasworks have closed, but the same pipes have remained in use for local distribution.

A similar overall pattern of development occurred with electricity. When first used in the 1870s and 1880s, mainly for lighting pub-

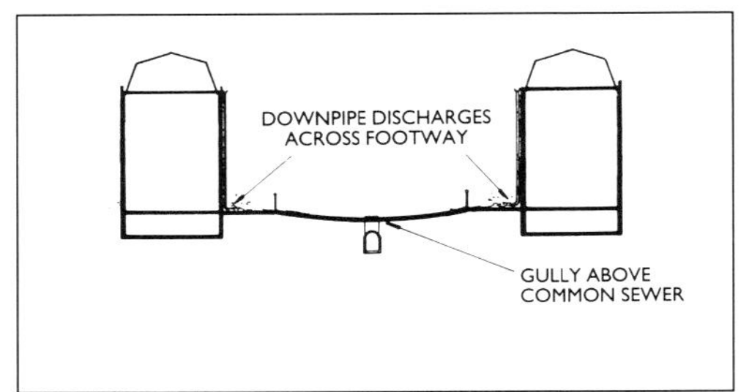

13

13. Typical London street at
the end of the 17th century, showing
the position of the services.
Alan Baxter & Associates.

14. The services infrastructure beneath
Holborn Viaduct, a street improvement
of 1863-9. In this project, the services
were carried in tunnels large enough
to be walked through.
Guidhall Library, London.

14 lic buildings and shops, electricity was generated locally, often by separate installations for each building. Transmission between buildings was by wires fixed to the rooftops. However, it was not long before electricity companies, like the gas companies before them, obtained the right to dig up the street to lay underground cables. London was notorious for its ill-coordinated and small-scale system of electrical supply, and for the political obstructions that were put in the way of large-scale electrical operators of the American or German type. In 1913, Chicago and Berlin each had six large generating stations: London, by contrast, had sixty-four.[7] It was not until after the First World War that this confusion was remedied. London then became linked to a national system of electrical distribution, and this has led ultimately to the closure of most of London's power stations. The only two that remain generate power exclusively for the London Underground.

With water, gas and electricity, the gradual introduction of large scale undertakings, whether private or publicly owned, eliminated the absurdity of rival services digging up the street to lay their pipes and cables. Although all of these services have been returned to the private sector during the last fifteen years, local competition has seldom reasserted itself. With telephones and telecommunications the opposite is true. The telephone system became virtually a government monopoly at the beginning of the present century, and this only ceased in the 1980s. The privatisation of the telephone agency, followed by the introduction of competition under an extremely liberal licensing policy, has brought a telecommunications revolution to London's streets. The sight of the road, or even more likely the pavement, being dug up by yet another cable company is now as much a feature of London life as the disruption caused by rival water companies in the 18th century.

The chaos caused by the insertion or renewal of infrastructure in the street is symptomatic of the problem which a city like London faces. More and more, the City is dependent on what lies beneath the ground, whether it be the underground railways, the services infrastructure, or the foundations on which its buildings stand. Yet each new insertion in the ground limits the freedom of future generations to reshape the City, and thus renew its vitality.[8] Until now, the conventional belief has been that a city with a complex underground existence is the natural product of a sophisticated and ingenious

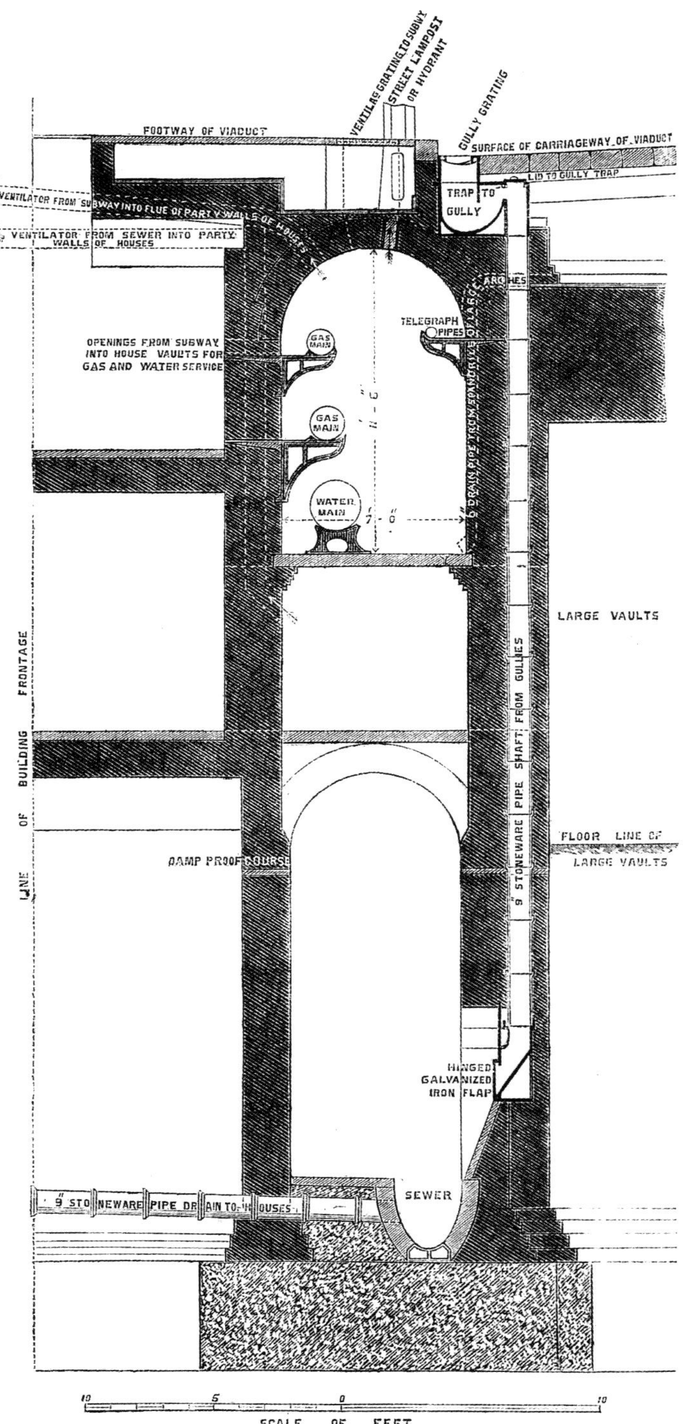

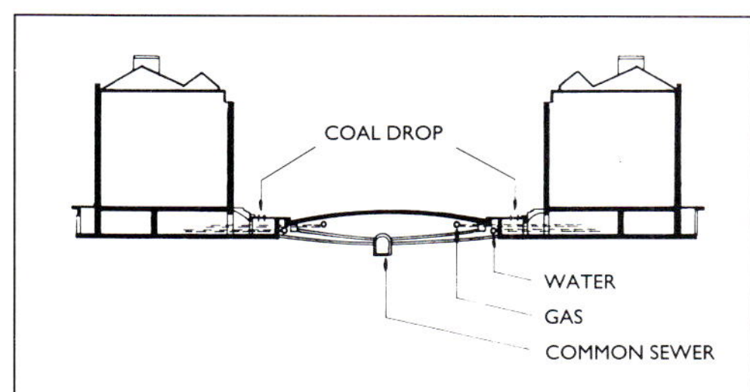

15

15. Typical London street in mid 19th century, showing the position of the services.
Alan Baxter & Associates.

16. Gas and water mains being laid in 1825, a watercolour by George Scharf. At that date, both gas and water mains were cast iron. Gas connections to buildings were always straight, whereas water connections made of lead could be shaped or bent.

17. The network of underground tunnels at King's Cross. The proposal to build an international station for the Channel Tunnel Rail Link, shown here, was dropped in 1992.
Alan Baxter & Associates.

society; that like a luxury ocean liner, it is bound to have a life below decks. However, there comes a time, which London may soon be reaching, when to add more to what is already in the ground begins to destroy, rather than improve, the quality of life above ground.

1. Bill Luckin, *Pollution and Control. A Social History of the Thames in the Nineteenth Century* (Bristol, 1986).
2. A. Morley Davies "London's First Conduit System: A Topographical Study," *Transactions of the London and Middlesex Topographical Society*, Vol. II (1913), pp. 9-59.
3. For instance, *The Letters of Monsieur César de Saussure to his Family* (edited by Madame Van Muyden, 1902), pp. 155-6.
4. Anne Hardy, "Water and the Search for Public Health in London in the 18th and 19th Centuries," *Medical History*, Vol. 28 (1984), pp. 262-3.
5. Denis Smith, "Sir Joseph William Bazalgette 1819-1891: Engineer to the Metropolitan Board of Works," *Transactions of the Newcomen Society*, Vol. 58 (1986-7), pp. 89-112.
6. Samuel Clegg Jr., *A Practical Treatise on the Manufacture and Distribution of Coal-Gas*, (2nd edition, 1853), p. 223.
7. Thomas P Hughes, *Networks of Power. Electrification in Western Society 1880-1930* (Baltimore and London, 1983), pp. 227, 257.
8. R.J.M. Sutherland, "Active Engineering History," *Structural Engineer*, Vol. 72 (5th July 1994), pp. 211-2.

16

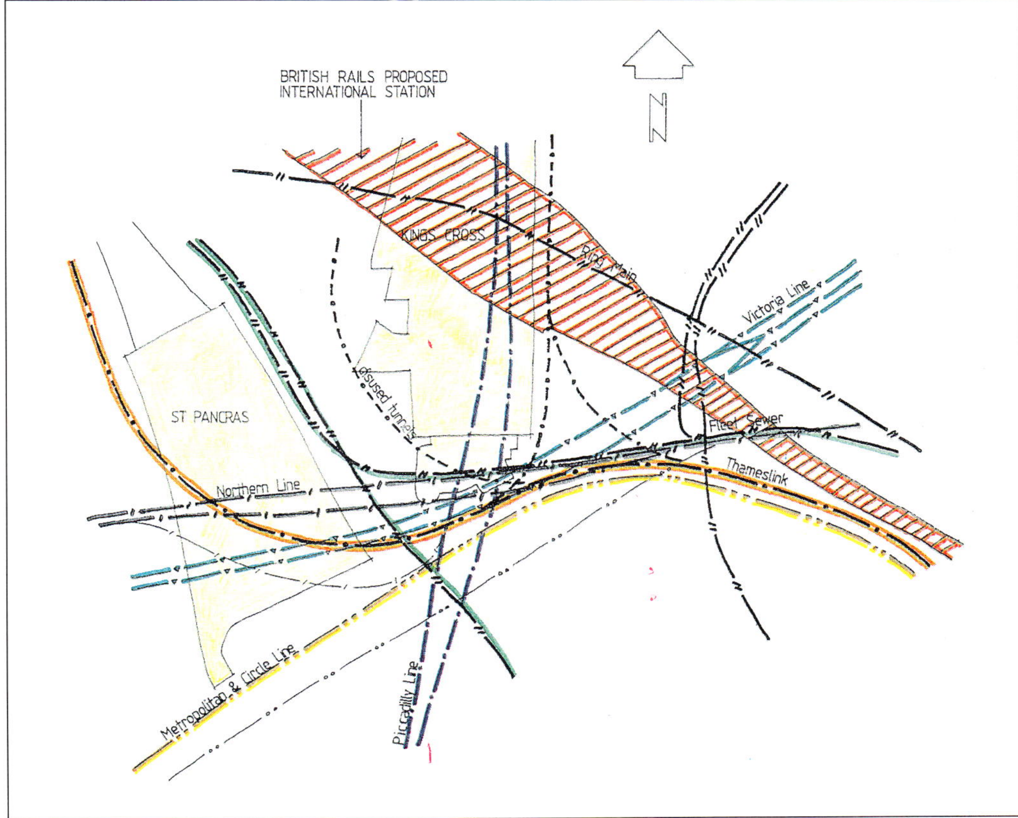

17

The images of this article are taken from: K. Garland, *Mr Beck's Underground Map* (Harrow Weald: Capital Transport Publishing, 1994).

1. Henry C Beck, original sketch for the London Underground diagram, 1931. One notes the significant features of all the future versions of the design: simplification of the route lines to verticals, horizontals or diagonals; the expansion of the central area; the elimination of all surface detail except for the line of the river Thames, itself presented in the same stylised form as the route lines (see fig. 5 on p. 19).

2. Beck in 1965.

On the following pages:

3. 1932 map which included the District Railway's route eastward as far as Barking, with the result that the central area was now so compressed that the detail there was too small to provide any useful information.

4. Stingemore's last card folder, produced in 1932. There was a slight expansion of the central area in comparison with his 1926 version.

5. Presentation visual of the diagram, 1931. This was at first rejected, and then accepted the following year as the basis for a trial printing (see fig. 1 on p. 16).

6. Quad royal poster of 1935. A most peculiar aberration, incorporating features imposed on Beck by the Board.

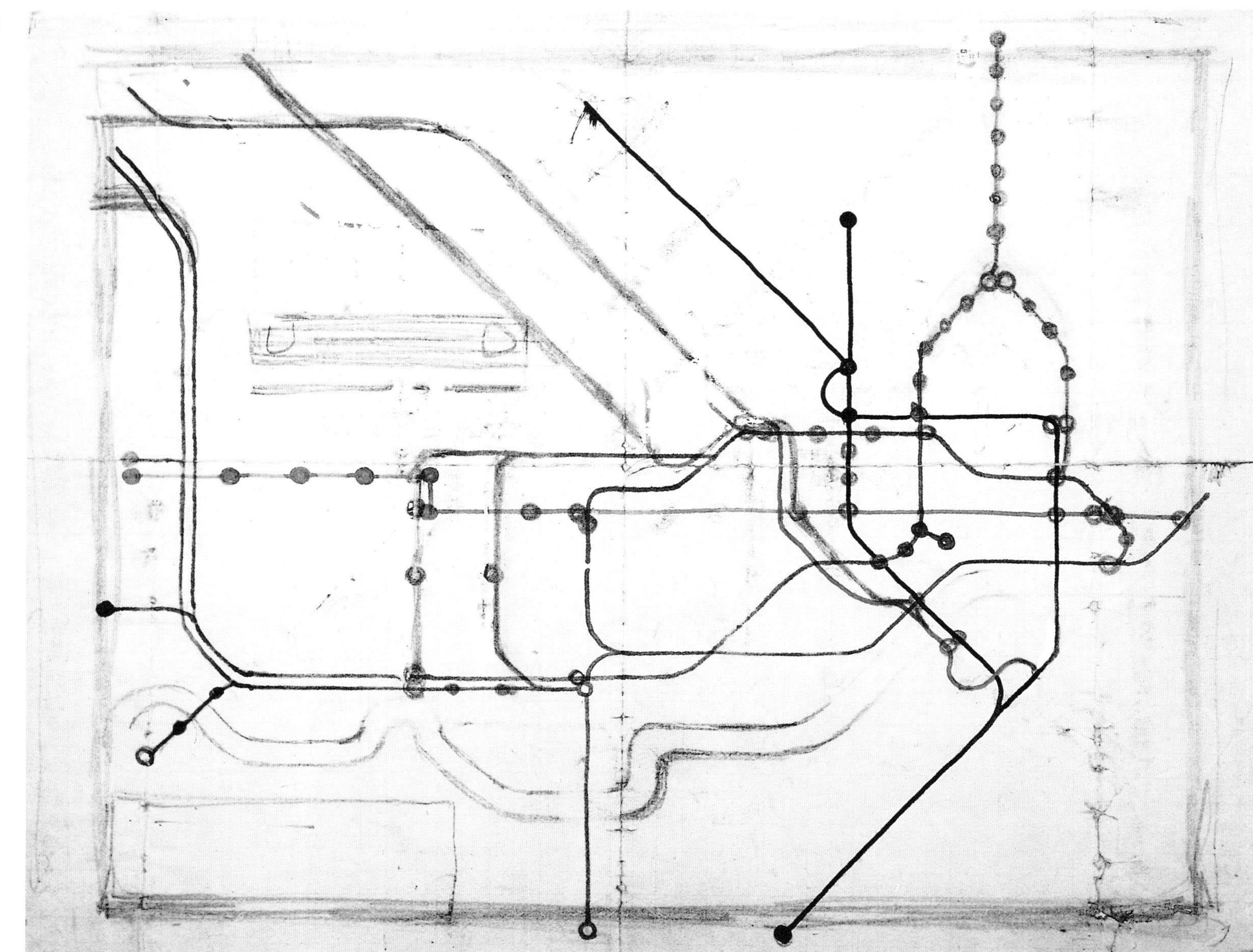

Henry C Beck and the London Underground Diagram

In January 1933 there appeared in London a new kind of transit map – a diagrammatic representation, in pocket folder form, of the seven Underground railway lines which were to become the responsibility of the newly appointed London Passenger Transport Board (LPTB). Though designated to take office formally on 1 July of that year, it was already in *de facto* control, as the nationalised inheritor of the Underground Group, founded in 1907 to consolidate the interests of a hitherto quarrelsome number of competing underground railways.

It is very probable that the Underground Group/LPTB remained sceptical of the usefulness of this novel route map, right up to the point when they put in hand the first edition. When its inventor, an unemployed engineering draughtsman named Henry C Beck (Harry to his friends) had first presented the idea to them in 1931, it had been flatly rejected. "Too revolutionary", they had said, tersely, handing his visual back to him without further comment.

But whatever reservations the LPTB may have had before publication of the new design, they were rapidly dispelled by the reaction of London's travelling public. Within one month they had devoured every one of the 750,000 copies of the first edition and a further 100,000 had to be rushed through the press in February. More reprints and new editions of the folder appeared throughout 1933; so many that it is certain there were at least 1.5 million copies issued during the first 12 months of its existence, not to speak of the many thousands of large poster editions of the same design displayed outside and inside every station of the Underground network.

What made the Diagram so popular? Why did everyone take so quickly to such an uncompromising and unfamiliar design? The British public, then as now, was not known to embrace innovation in visual matters, yet they appear to have harboured none of the suspicions earlier displayed by the LPTB.

Perhaps the best answer to this question lies in the character and background of the inventor himself. Beck was a typical, commuting Londoner with a thorough, down-to-earth training in technical drawing and no aesthetic pretensions. Along with millions of fellow-commuters he had experienced the confusion and ambiguities present in existing maps of the Underground; whenever he attempted a journey at variance with his usual, daily one, he was forced to pore over them, teasing out the information he needed about interchange

2

points from the pseudo-geographic congestion of the central part of the network ("pseudo-" because, despite appearances, the predecessors to Beck's Diagram were not topographically accurate – they only attempted to look as though they were).

However, whereas his fellow-travellers had no choice but to put up with the inadequacies of the Underground route maps, Beck had the skill, the vision and – due to his enforced idleness as an unemployed person – the time to devise an alternative. In an account of his own life at the time, written in 1968 at the request of the present writer, he described his conception of the Diagram thus: "Looking at the old map of the Underground railways, it occurred to me that it might be possible to tidy it up by straightening the lines, experimenting with diagonals and evening out the distance between stations. The more I thought about it the more convinced I became that the idea was worth trying, so, selecting the Central London Railway as my horizontal base line I made a rough sketch. I tried to imagine that I was using a convex lens or mirror, so as to present the central area on a larger scale. This, I thought, would give a needed clarity to interchange information."

From an initial sketch Beck progressed to a careful presentation visual. As his account stated he had taken the Central London Railway as a horizontal based line, round which he erected a network of horizontals, verticals and diagonals. By compressing the outlying parts of the routes he was able (a) to include the whole of them except the eastern part of the District Railway beyond Whitechapel, and (b)

to enlarge the central portion of the network. At this stage he still employed blobs to denote stations as had his predecessors, with rings to differentiate interchange stations.

Though deeply disappointed by the rejection already mentioned, Beck was not prepared to let the matter rest there. Supported by colleagues (one of whom, F H Stingemore, was the designer of the most recent card folder maps yet who, generously, recognised the superior merits of Beck's design) he persisted: "About a year later [in 1932, that is] I had another look at the drawing, and decided, without much hope, to try again. This time Mr Patmore of the Publicity Department sent for me... and greeted me with the words, 'You'd better sit down. I'm going to give you a shock. We're going to print it!'. Thus it was, and only, I believe though my pertinacity, that the London Underground Diagram was born."

The first proof of the Diagram, in card folder form, resembled the presentation visual closely, one significant difference being that, at interchange stations, rings were replaced by outline diamonds; a motif that was to recur, with variations, for some years afterwards. Before publication, however, Beck had refined the blobs used to denote non-interchange stations, substituting a much more appropriate device, called by him a "tick", extending at ninety degrees from the route line itself and pointing directly at the station name. This was a small but important refinement, lightening the Diagram overall and giving it a more elegant appearance.

There is some uncertainty about the debut of the Diagram. Beck's own account, written long after the event, states: "Even after the idea was accepted the Publicity Manager was not any too sure about it, and decided to give it a trial run, inviting the travelling public to comment on the new format."

A "trial run" could be taken to be a few hundreds – and that was, indeed, Beck's recollection of the number initially printed; but there are no records of such an initial quantity having been printed, although there is the intriguing evidence of the following phrase on the front cover of the first edition: "A new design for an old map. We should welcome your comments. Please write to Publicity Manager, 55 Broadway, London SW1." One suspects this was probably a leftover from just such a trial printing as Beck described. It would, surely, be a strange request to appear for the first time on an edition of 750,000, since by that time the LPTB were well and truly committed to the design.

18

UNDERGROUND
MAP OF LONDON
REFERENCE
DISTRICT RAILWAY
BAKERLOO LINE AND
LONDON L.M.S. THROUGH SERVICES
ELECTRIC PICCADILLY LINE AND
RAILWAY DISTRICT RLY THROUGH SERVICES
HIGHGATE & HAMPSTEAD LINE
CITY & SOUTH LONDON RAILWAY
CENTRAL LONDON RAILWAY
METROPOLITAN RAILWAY
EAST LONDON RAILWAY
EXCHANGE STATIONS
Copies of this Map can be obtained
free upon application to
ASSISTANT PUBLICITY MANAGER,
55, Broadway, Westminster, S.W.1.

3

TO
Kenton
Harrow & Wealdstone
Headstone Lane
Hatch End for Pinner
Carpenders Park
Bushey and Oxhey
Watford (High Street)
Watford Junction
TO
Harrow
Uxbridge and
Rickmansworth
TO
Bounds Green
Arnos Grove
Southgate
Enfield West
Cockfosters
TO
Stepney Green
Mile End
Bow Road
Bromley
West Ham
Plaistow
Upton Park
East Ham
Barking and
Southend
TO
Sudbury Hill
South Harrow
Rayners Lane
Eastcote
Ruislip Manor
Ruislip
Ickenham
Hillingdon
and Uxbridge
TO
Boston Manor
Osterley
Hounslow East
Hounslow Central
Hounslow West
EDGWARE
BURNT OAK (WATLING)
COLINDALE
HENDON CENTRAL
BRENT
GOLDERS GREEN
WOOD GREEN
TURNPIKE LANE
HIGHGATE
FINSBURY PARK
MANOR HOUSE
PRESTON ROAD
WEMBLEY PARK
NORTH WEMBLEY
NEASDEN & KINGSBURY
DOLLIS HILL
WEST HAMPSTEAD
HAMPSTEAD
GILLESPIE ROAD
HOLLOWAY ROAD
DRAYTON PARK
TUFNELL PARK
KENTISH TOWN
CALEDONIAN ROAD
HIGHBURY & ISLINGTON
WEMBLEY FOR SUDBURY
WILLESDEN GREEN
KILBURN & BRONDESBURY
FINCHLEY ROAD
SWISS COTTAGE
BELSIZE PARK
CHALK FARM
CAMDEN TOWN
MORNINGTON CRESCENT
YORK ROAD
CANONBURY & ESSEX ROAD
SUDBURY TOWN
STONEBRIDGE PARK
ALPERTON
HARLESDEN
KENSAL GREEN
QUEENS PARK
KILBURN PARK
MAIDA VALE
MARLBORO ROAD
ST JOHNS WOOD
BAKER STREET
GREAT PORTLAND STREET
EUSTON
KINGS CROSS ST PANCRAS
ANGEL
OLD STREET
PARK ROYAL
NORTH ACTON
WILLESDEN JUNCTION (NEW STATION)
WESTBOURNE PARK
WARWICK AVENUE
REGENTS PARK
EDGWARE ROAD
MARYLEBONE
BISHOPS ROAD
WARREN ST
GOODGE ST
RUSSELL SQ
BRITISH MUSEUM
FARRINGDON
ALDERSGATE
MOORGATE
CHANCERY LANE
POST OFFICE
LIVERPOOL STREET
WHITECHAPEL (FOR E. LONDON RLY)
WEST ACTON For Hanger Hill
EAST ACTON
WOOD LANE
LADBROKE GROVE
ROYAL OAK
PADDINGTON
PRAED ST
QUEENS ROAD
LANCASTER GATE
MARBLE ARCH
BOND ST
OXFORD CIRCUS
TOTTENHAM COURT RD
HOLBORN
ALDWYCH
COVENT GARDEN
MANSION HOUSE
BANK
ALDGATE EAST
MARK LANE
ALDGATE
ST MARY'S
NORTH EALING
EALING BROADWAY
EALING COMMON
ACTON TOWN
SOUTH ACTON
LATIMER ROAD
UXBRIDGE ROAD
BAYSWATER
NOTTING HILL GATE
HOLLAND PARK
SHEPHERDS BUSH
PICCADILLY
LEICESTER SQUARE
STRAND (FOR B ST)
TEMPLE
BLACKFRIARS
CANNON STREET
MONUMENT
LONDON BRIDGE
SOUTH EALING
NORTHFIELDS
CHISWICK PARK
TURNHAM GREEN
RAVENSCOURT PARK
GOLDHAWK ROAD
ADDISON ROAD
EARLS COURT
HIGH STREET KENSINGTON
GLOUCESTER ROAD
KNIGHTSBRIDGE
BROMPTON ROAD
HYDE PARK CORNER
DOVER ST
TRAFALGAR SQUARE
CHARING CROSS
WESTMINSTER
WATERLOO
LAMBETH NORTH
ELEPHANT & CASTLE
BOROUGH
STAMFORD BROOK
GUNNERSBURY
BARONS COURT
HAMMERSMITH
WEST KENSINGTON
WEST BROMPTON
SOUTH KENSINGTON
SLOANE SQUARE
VICTORIA
ST JAMES PARK
KENNINGTON
KEW GARDENS
WALHAM GREEN
PARSONS GREEN
PUTNEY BRIDGE
EAST PUTNEY
SOUTHFIELDS
WIMBLEDON PARK
WIMBLEDON
RIVER THAMES
OVAL
STOCKWELL
CLAPHAM NORTH
CLAPHAM COMMON
CLAPHAM SOUTH
BALHAM
TRINITY ROAD (TOOTING BEC)
TOOTING BROADWAY
COLLIERS WOOD
SOUTH WIMBLEDON (MERTON)
MORDEN
FOR OPENING DATES
OF PICCADILLY RAILWAY
EXTENSIONS SEE BACK.
UNDERGROUND
RAILWAYS OF LONDON
REFERENCE
District Railway
London Electric Railway Bakerloo Line
Piccadilly Line
Hampstead and Highgate Line
City and South London Rly.
Central London Railway
Metropolitan Railway
Metropolitan Railway (Great Northern and City Section)
Interchange Stations
THE DAVID ALLEN PRINTING CO (LONDON) LTD

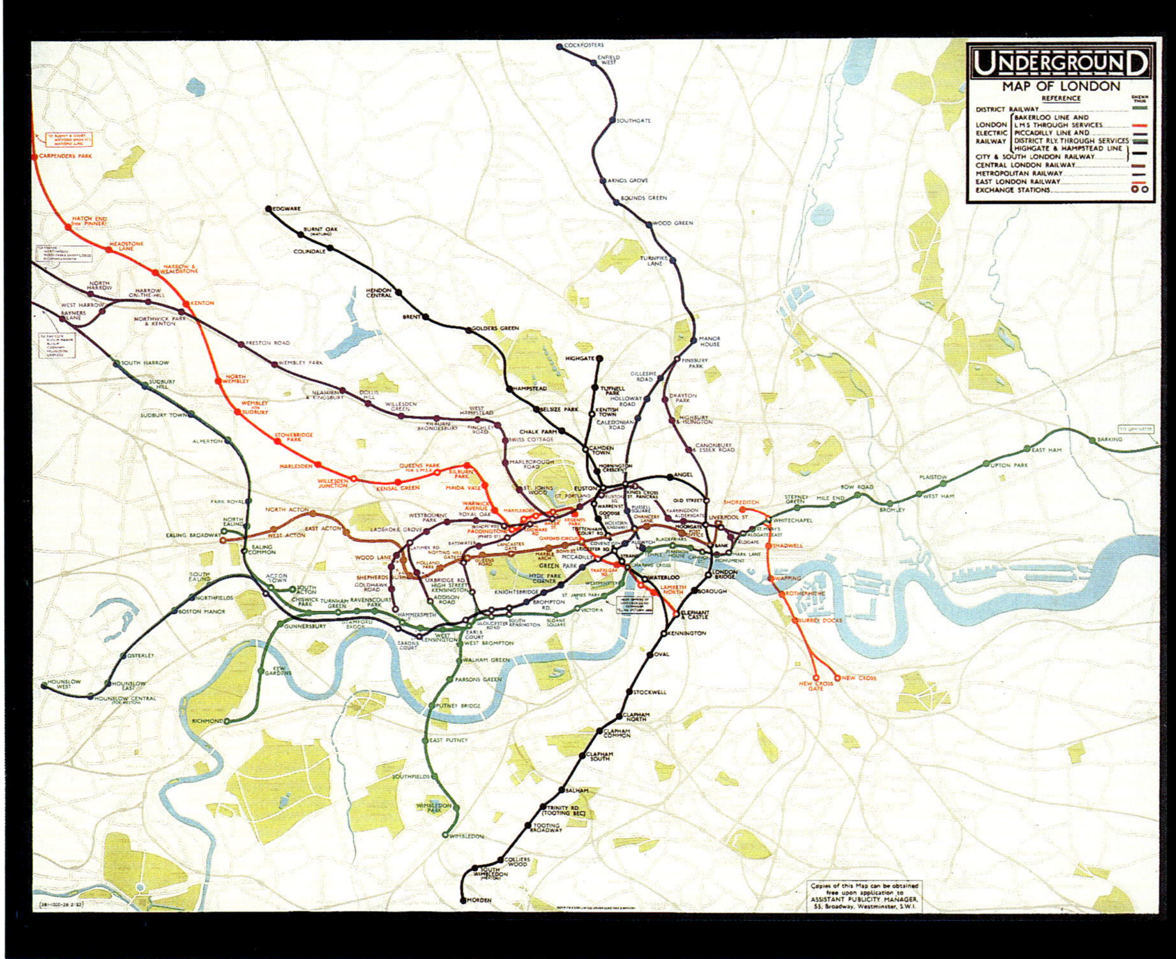

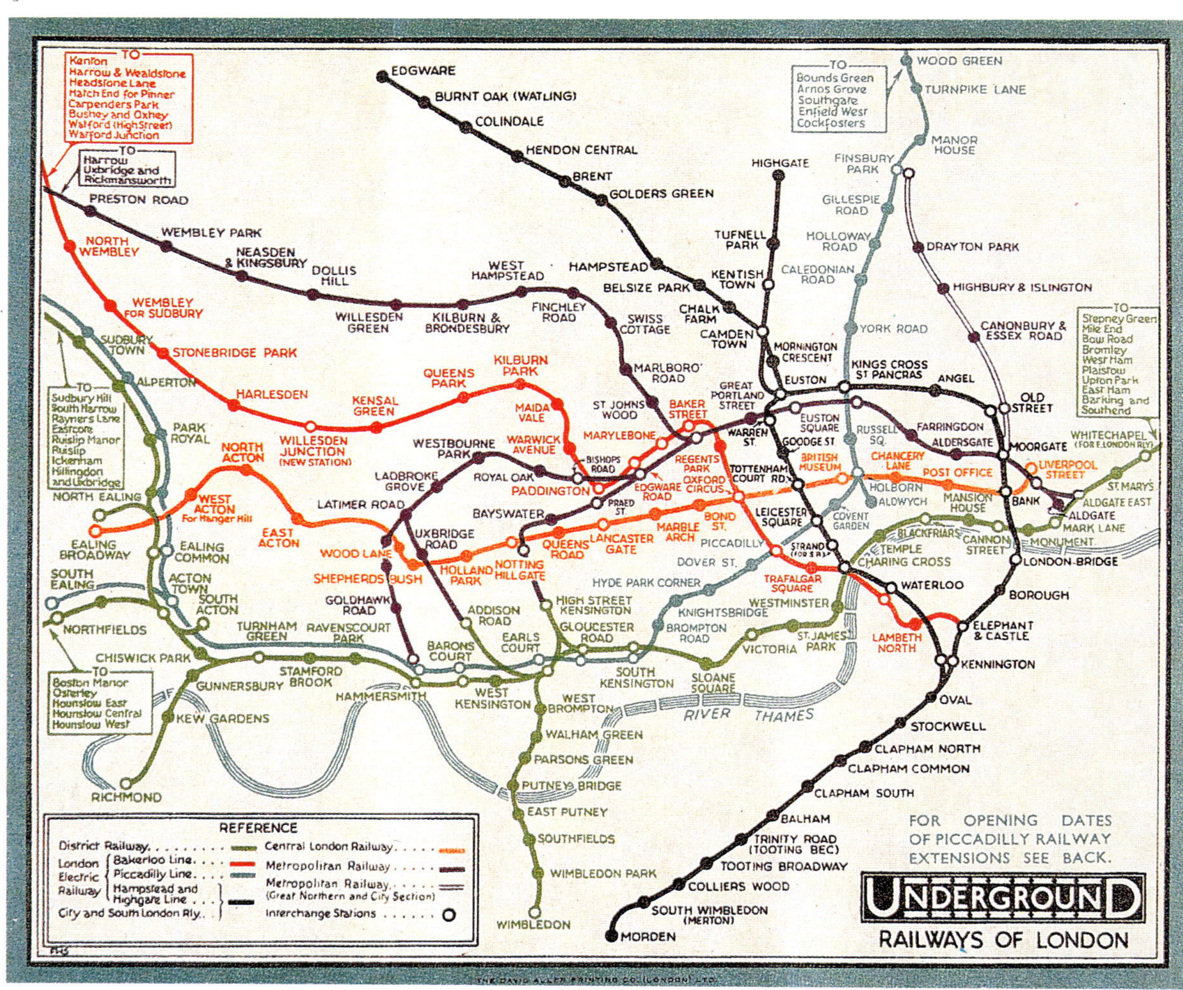

4

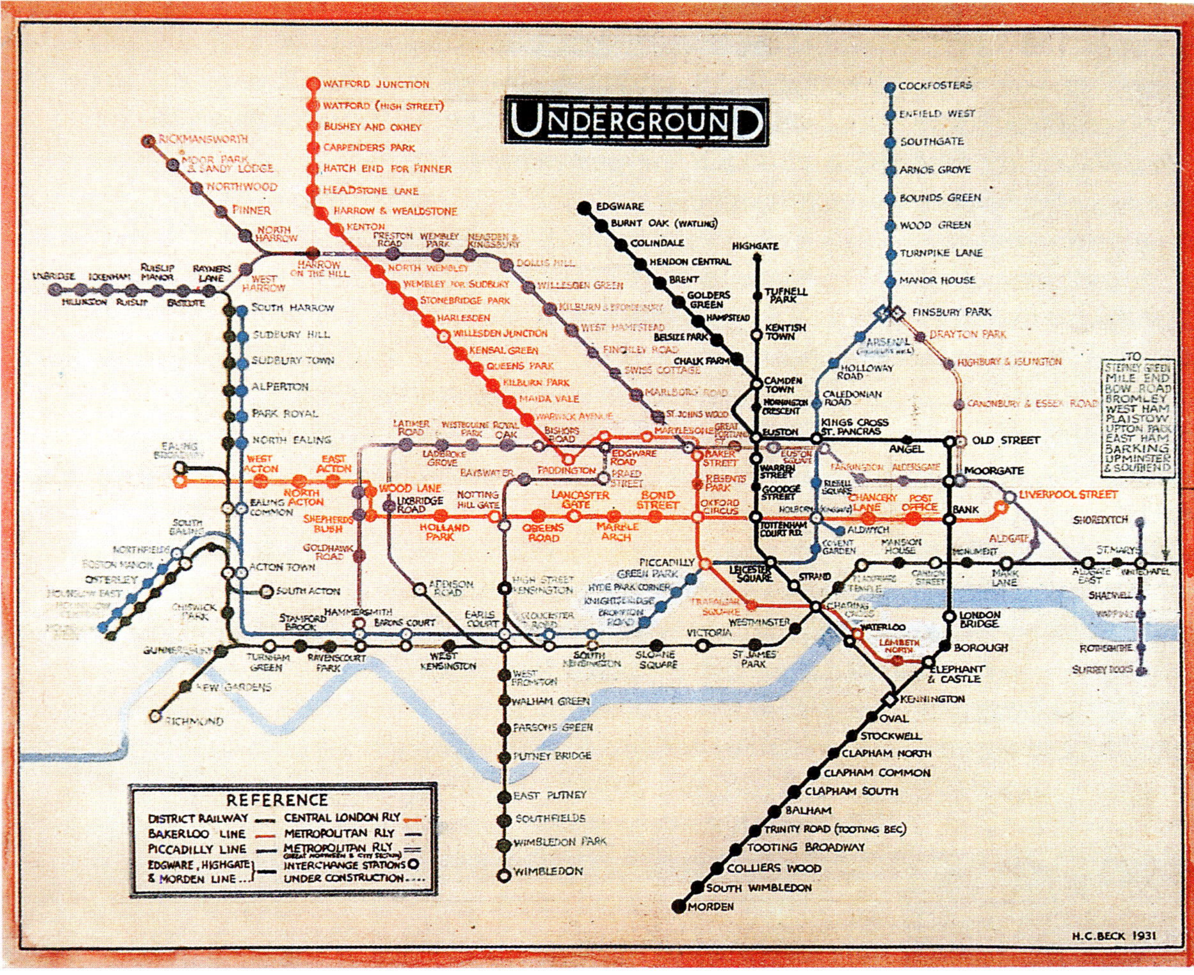

UNDERGROUND
REFERENCE
DISTRICT RAILWAY
BAKERLOO LINE
PICCADILLY LINE
EDGWARE, HIGHGATE & MORDEN LINE
CENTRAL LONDON RLY
METROPOLITAN RLY
METROPOLITAN RLY (GREAT NORTHERN & CITY SECTION)
INTERCHANGE STATIONS
UNDER CONSTRUCTION
H.C.BECK 1931

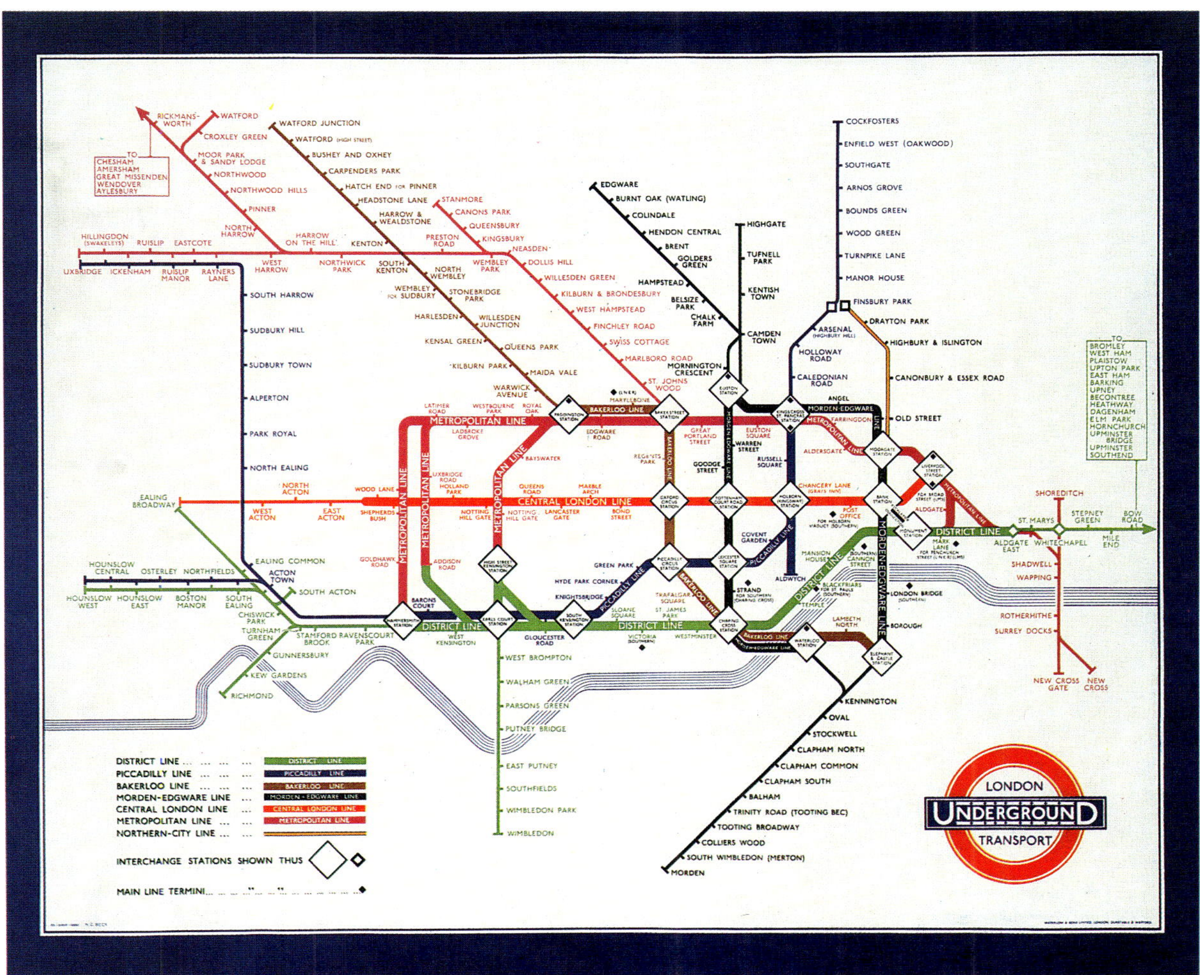

LONDON UNDERGROUND TRANSPORT
DISTRICT LINE
PICCADILLY LINE
BAKERLOO LINE
MORDEN-EDGWARE LINE
CENTRAL LONDON LINE
METROPOLITAN LINE
NORTHERN-CITY LINE
INTERCHANGE STATIONS SHOWN THUS
MAIN LINE TERMINI

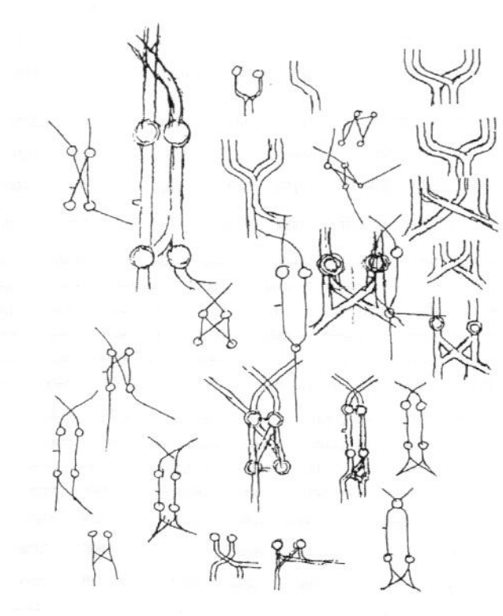

7, 9. Pencil sketches by Beck of the Camden Town/Mornington Crescent/ Euston complex, made in 1960 during work on an unpublished design he submitted unsuccessfully to London Transport. It was virtually impossible to represent it on the diagram in any but the most rudimentary form.

8. Map of London Underground at real scale, with vertical dashed lines indicating the ever greater total areas encompassed between 1908 and 1959.

20

Not only was the Diagram a huge success as a useful piece of information design; it became, almost overnight, an icon for London itself. Thus, though conceived as no more than a common-sense device, intended to help Underground travellers get on at the right station, make the right connections and get off at the right destination, it was seen as something else as well. In their hands was a small miracle: an orderly simulacrum of a disorderly, disjointed collection of urban villages, only barely discernible from one another on the ground, yet possessed with all the pride and exclusiveness of true communities. For the first time, perhaps, it all began to make some kind of sense.

Some critics protested that the Diagram was an inaccurate and unreliable guide to London's complex configuration; as few even hinted it might be part of a devious plot to fool a gullible public into thinking the remoter stations on the Underground were more accessible than in fact they were. But the public were not under any illusion, either about the nature of their vast city or the true distances between outly-ing stations on their Underground network. The Diagram represented a view of London and its Underground that they had – albeit unconsciously – been looking out for; one that would cope with the information needs of a growing population now committed to travelling considerable distances every day from the new suburbs, and of visitors from the provinces making their first, timorous acquaintance with the metropolis in increasing numbers throughout the 1930s.

More than that, it was an optimistic vision of a city that was not chaotic, in spite of appearances to the contrary, that knew what it was about and wanted its visitors to know it, too. Its bright, clean and colourful design exuded confidence in every line. Once it burst on their gaze, Londoners and their visitors could not imagine how they got along without it.

The status of the Diagram was confirmed by the arrival, in March 1933, of the poster version. Free of the confines of the pocket folder format, Beck produced a design of such refinement and simple grace that has never been surpassed. Undoubtedly, one reason for its classic quality was the required use of the "Underground Railway Sans" typeface specially designed by the famous calligrapher Edward Johnston. Paradoxically, it was just the sort of typeface, having generously shaped characters requiring equally generous spacing between them, that most diagram designers would recoil from in dismay as being far too unwieldy for this purpose, especially since its use was restricted to capital letters only. But Beck, exercising all his ingenuity and patience, handled them with consummate skill. Though those who followed him were able to employ the more compact lower-case letters of the Johnston typeface, he demonstrated triumphantly, throughout his 27-year stewardship of his Diagram, that he could make a virtue out of an awkward necessity.

The advent of the poster version produced the first known reaction to Beck's invention from Frank Pick, Chief Executive of the LPTB, in the form of a memorandum to his Publicity Manager dated 3 August 1933: "I

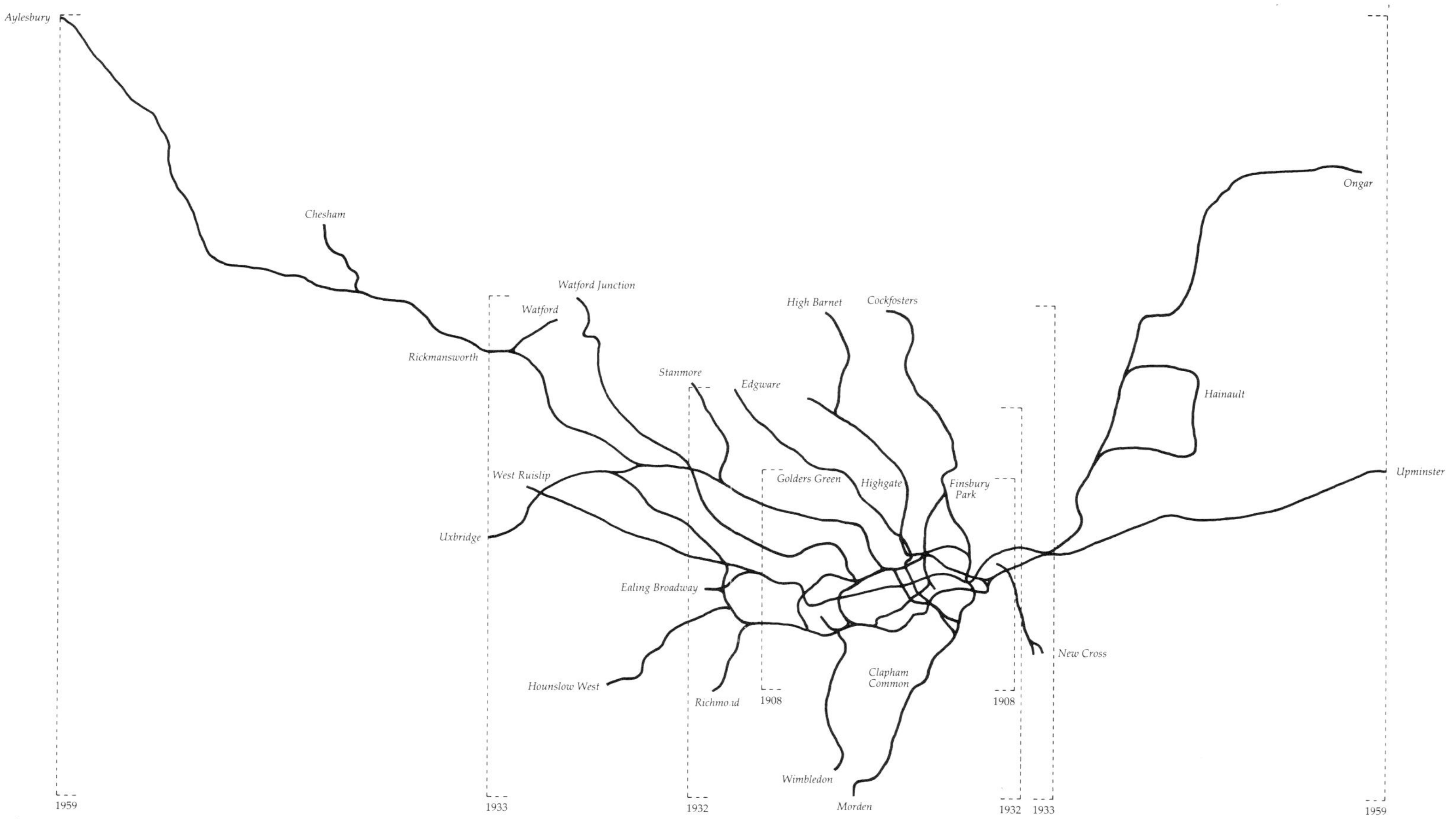

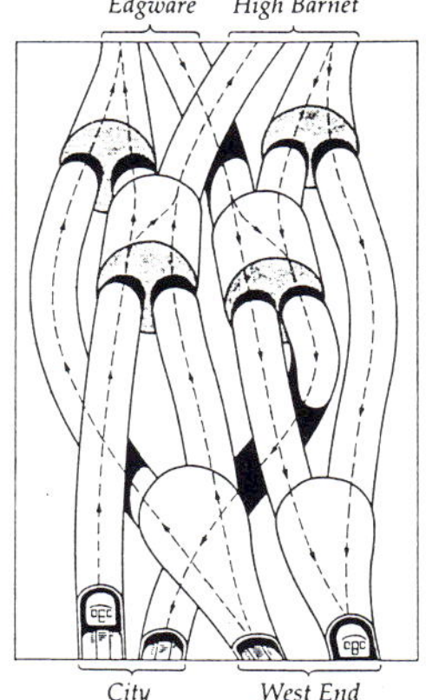

9

had a look at your quad royal map. I confess that upon a large scale this looks very convenient and tidy and is a better map than any we have had so far."

That Pick felt it necessary to "confess" hints strongly at an earlier lack of enthusiasm, and his phrase "convenient and tidy" is hardly wholehearted praise for an invention of genius. Yet Pick was known throughout his long career, first with the Underground Group, later with the London Passenger Transport Board, as a vigorous patron of artists, architects and designers (he, after all had originally commissioned the design of Johnston's Sans-Serif typeface in 1913). It seems inexplicably strange that he paid no more than a passing interest in the design that came to symbolise so much of what the LPTB stood for under his leadership.

Not that Beck was left to work on his subsequent versions of the Diagram unmolested. Even Pick's nominal boss, Lord Ashfield, Chairman of the LPTB, was not averse to suggesting "improvements", as did other senior members of the staff. One of the more foolish proposals which Beck had to take seriously, much as he disapproved of it, involved enlarging the diamonds representing the central interchange stations and squeezing the actual names of the stations *inside* the diamonds. After he had managed, by the late 1930s, to get rid of that nonsense, he found himself faced with a scarcely credible demand from the Operating Department that interchange stations should be signified by pairs or triplets of interlinked rings and that the names of all stations serving two or three Underground lines should have their names duplicated or triplicated. The interlinked rings did not last beyond 1941 but he was stuck with the duplication and triplication of station names until 1946.

Persistence won the day eventually. From 1947 to 1959 Harry Beck had things more or less his own way with the Diagram. He was able to adapt the design towards a more rectilinear configuration, eliminating most of the diagonals. In this way he was able to achieve the ideal of a true Diagram, as far away from a topographically accurate original as possible with only the line of the River Thames and the North = up, South = down, West = left and East = right orientation remaining.

Beck was not to know, when he executed it, that his 1959 edition of the Diagram was the last he would ever be responsible for. He had always, from the very first edition, undertaken the work on a freelance basis, even when, from 1933 to 1946, he was also a full-

10

11

12

time employee of the LPTB. There was no written contract, but as the inventor of the Diagram he naturally assumed that he would either be commissioned to undertake all revisions, or be thoroughly consulted about them, so he was deeply shocked to discover, early in 1960, that someone else had usurped what he believed to be his rightful place and produced a dreadfully inadequate adaptation of his design; even more shocking was the discovery that the new version was credited to Harold F Hutchison, the Publicity Officer who, for the last few years, had been his closest inside contact; a man whom he had never known to possess any design skills.

Beck then began a long and fruitless exchange of letters with Hutchison and his superiors. There was even talk of possible legal action. But Beck had no financial resources, and in any case his wife, Nora, was deeply agitated by the dispute and wished it to be ended. Reluctantly, still bitter and thwarted at this betrayal by the LPTB, he was forced to concede defeat. The Hutchison design was generally recognised, within a year or so, to be a failure; but Beck was not asked to resume his stewardship of his own design. Instead, another member of the LPTB staff, Paul E Garbutt, undertook a more sensitive version which had much more of the spirit of Beck's original.

Harry Beck died in 1974, aged 73. In the last few years of his life he was happy to know that his great achievement had been fully recognised and honoured by his fellow designers. It is a pity, though, that he did not live long enough to receive the more public acclaim that would, by now, have been given to him by grateful Londoners.

There have been many attempts to emulate the splendid example Beck has given us, none of them as yet surpassing his own. I am quite sure we shall go on trying; if one of us should ever succeed, I am equally sure Harry would have been the first to acknowledge it. He was a generous soul.

21

13. Quad royal poster of 1940. Beck was confronted with three new requirements from the Board: to use interlinked rings for the interchange stations, to duplicate a large number of station names on the grounds that they served two Underground lines, to change diagonals from 45° to 60°.

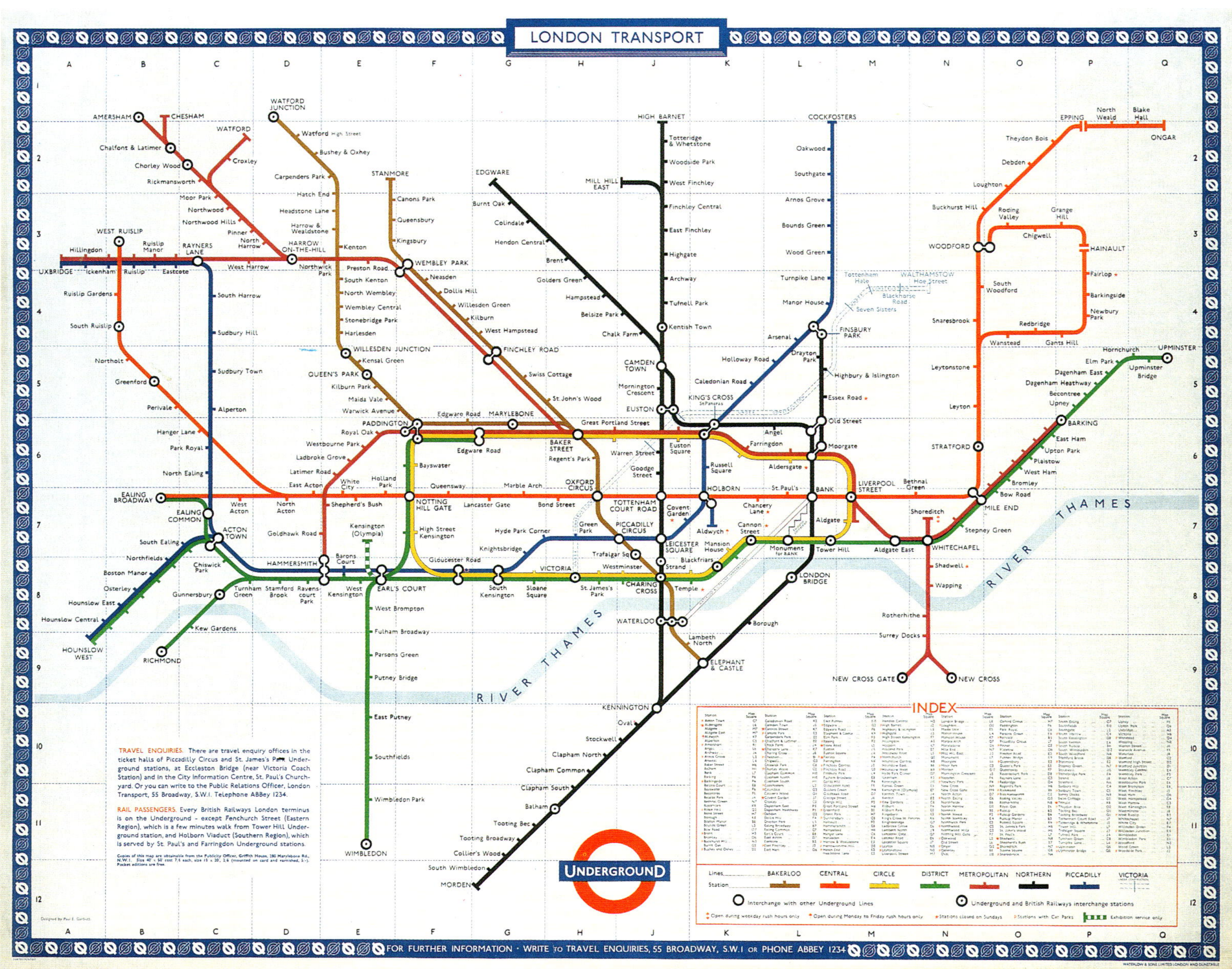

14. Quad royal poster "Designed by
Paul E. Garbutt", March 1964. Garbutt
created a distinctive shape for the
Circle Line, and introduced the black
dot within the standard interchange
ring. It still shared with its immediate
predecessor those close similarities
to the Beck diagram of 1933-8 which
clearly demonstrated its inspiration.

24 "I hoped to find modern architecture in London. I found only Lutyens – who is not modern. The only true modern construction is, taken as a whole, not architecture: the Underground. But this is more important for London than all the works of Lutyens and England's other famous architects put together. It is also very well managed. When it rains in London, posters rapidly appear saying, 'If you want to miss the rain, take the Underground.' If you want to miss the chaos of London's architecture, take the Underground too. There is no architecture about. In twenty minutes you can get out into the countryside…"[1]

In these words Steen Eiler Rasmussen, Danish architect-planner and author of the peerless *London. The Unique City*, reflected on his first visit to the British metropolis in 1927.

Rasmussen's wry remarks draw out strands that run through the whole idea of the London Underground. They convey, for a start, the glamour and allure that the Underground has always enjoyed in the eyes of foreigners. It is still the same. The jaundiced Londoner is used to troops of tourists crushing into tube trains all summer; what puzzles and amazes him, as he feigns sleep or shelters behind his newspaper, is that some of them seem to be riding the system "for the joy of the thing." Very few people do that on the New York subway or even the sumptuous Moscow metro.

Rasmussen expresses grateful relief, too, for the Underground efficiency, clarity and order, for the redemption and reintegration of London's chaos and sprawl (a task epitomized in the necessary lie of the admired Underground Map) and for the opportunities it offers for escape – escape from London itself. And finally, Rasmussen shares with his readers the joy of unearthing good modern architecture in an improbable context. In the buildings and design of the London Underground, he seems to say, British architecture abandons its wayward individualism and relaxes about belonging, simply and straightforwardly, to its own century.

This, then, is the myth of the London Underground. But what does the Underground mean in the life of London and for Londoners? Something more ambiguous and less exhilarating than it means for the visitor, certainly. Patience, respect, affection, pragmatism, antagonism, not a little fear: that is the cocktail of emotions that the habitual user feels for the Underground. Not a wholly positive image, perhaps. But it chimes in with the history of a system that has been evolving and elaborat-

1

ing in tandem with its unruly city for more than a century and a half. If London can boast the world's oldest underground railway, the record of that railway is shot through with memories both of heroism and of trauma.

The story of that heroism and trauma alike begins with the Thames Tunnel between Wapping and Rotherhithe (1825-43), the world's first completed underwater tunnel on a large scale. This vaunting essay in technological ambition was conceived during the most ebullient decade in London's history. Britain had vanquished Napoleon and stood material master of the world. To British engineers, anything then seemed to be possible – even tunnelling beneath the gravelly bed of the Thames. The brainchild of Sir Marc Brunel, the tunnel was built under the direction of his

celebrated son, Isambard Kingdom Brunel. Since in 1825 no public railways yet existed on the surface, let alone below ground, it was intended as a road crossing.

As a practical project the Thames Tunnel proved an abject failure. The tunnel was flooded out on three terrifying occasions; many workmen succumbed to disease contracted in the stinking, sewage-ridden atmosphere beneath the river, while others died in accidents. Even when the tunnel was finished, there was no money for the approach roads. The engineering prodigy that Schinkel and others came to marvel at during the halcyon days of its construction dwindled to a pedestrian route, where whores and sellers of trinkets hid in the half-light between the cross-arches and pestered tourists.

1. Sheltering on the escalators at Piccadilly Circus, 1940.

2. Henry Moore on the set of *Out of Chaos*, 1943, re-enacting his earlier visits to the tube shelters.

One French visitor's reaction is typical: "One feels that one would die if one had to spend even a couple of hours in this hypogeum, where the perpetually dripping water forms large black, viscous puddles under foot [...] There are puppet shows and concertina players, pathetic but hopeless attempts at enlivening this burial crypt [...] It is patent that trade here is only a thin cloak for prostitution."[2]

In 1869 the Thames Tunnel was taken over by a railway and in due course annexed into one of the Underground's least frequented branches, between Whitechapel and New Cross. It is now (in 1996) to be relined, after a bitter and prolonged battle between conservationists and the transport authorities.

A harsh and discouraging beginning, then. Yet the Thames Tunnel gave prophetic substance, method and character to the Underground idea. It proved that tunnels of wide bore could be dug not just through the deep beds of clay upon which most of London stands but even beneath the treacherous sand and gravel of London's river. The shield method which Marc Brunel and Henry Maudslay devised for driving forward the tunnel, inch by inch, would in perfected and mechanized form bore the tunnels of the deep-level, electric railways in the years around 1900; the same principle continues for underground tunnels the world over today. The Brunels' parallel, twin-tunnel system also became the hallmark of those later "tubular railways" or tubes – more claustrophobic yet more dramatic than the two-track, cut-and-cover tunnels of the first underground railway.

As for those who touted their wares in the early Thames Tunnel, their troglodytic lifestyle was all too familiar. So many of London's Victorian poor toiled and slept in cellars and basements that their colonization of the Brunel arches must have seemed distasteful but unsurprising. In the 1930s, when the authorities first began to frown upon basement living, more than one hundred thousand Londoners still slept beneath pavement level.[3]

Not until that same, slum-clearing decade, and not by coincidence, did the suburban ends of the tubes begin to thrust upwards and outwards into open space. Until then many Londoners inhabited dark places and went about their business under smoke-ridden skies, accustomed to shadows, not stars. To that extent, underground culture was rooted in the life of Victorian London.

The story of London's first underground railway proper begins in the 1850s. It was the outcome of efforts by a man as tenacious as

2

the Brunels, the City of London's official solicitor, Charles Pearson. His vision was pragmatic: to relieve city streets by getting freight traffic below ground. But Pearson hoped also to draw working-class Londoners out of the overcrowded centre towards the healthier suburbs – a recurrent theme in London's history. Neither he nor his supporters planned that such a railway should serve London as a whole. The original Metropolitan Railway, built between Paddington and Farringdon in 1860-3, was meant to be a feeder line connecting the main-line termini of Paddington, St Pancras and King's Cross with the City of London, Smithfield Market and, in due course, districts south of the Thames.

The Metropolitan proved a quick and unexpected success for local passenger traffic.

Only then did the vision of the Underground enlarge into that of an integrated route describing a great elliptical loop round the metropolis with feeders off, allowing passengers to move conveniently into and about central and western London. This loop, constructed in 1865-71 but completed only in 1882, came to be called the Inner Circle.

To prevent monopoly, Parliament insisted that the line should be divided between two separate companies, so setting up confusions of nomenclature and working which later integrations have never quite expunged. To this day, only the true Underground aficionado is able to explain the difference between Metropolitan and District Line timetables and rolling stock and the mode of their interaction on the Circle Line. Thus did the pattern of the

26 London Underground emerge: a series of empirical, fragmented initiatives bound slowly together into a city-wide, autonomous system.

As a feat of engineering the first Underground was nothing like the titanic struggle of the Thames Tunnel. The chosen method of excavation, cut-and-cover, was well known to the railway-builders of the 1860s. But the scale and the urban topography of the line did raise new technical problems: widespread demolitions of property (particularly during the later stages of the line through the City of London), the construction of abutment walls of a thickness not seen in railway-building before (to avoid compensation claims for subsidence of adjoining properties), the diversion of traffic where the line was built beneath major roads, and the need to work around London's intensifying infrastructure.

For years the streets were in chaos. In 1862 the Fleet Sewer burst, setting the work back by months. All this explains why other cities thinking about urban transport at the time, beginning with New York, opted for the environmental disaster of rackety elevated railways along their streets. That at least London was spared.

The engineers to both the Metropolitan and the District companies were the experienced and steady John Fowler (later joint engineer for the Forth Bridge) and his assistant, T.M. Johnson. Theirs were the first underground station buildings: modest single-storey, yellow-brick structures in Italian taste which reminded one early passenger of "isolated police stations, or half an establishment for baths and wash-houses." Below ground, a few of the early stations (notably Baker Street) were in ill-ventilated tunnels; others were open and covered with iron and glass roof arching over the platforms – later removed. The same observer found his station "not a very cheerful place [...] A roof of corrugated iron and glass, columns and tie-rods of the same material, walls decorated with that species of light literature which sets forth the merits of cutlery, sixteen-shilling trousers, and restorative elixir, is not calculated to cheer the heart of man above ground."[4]

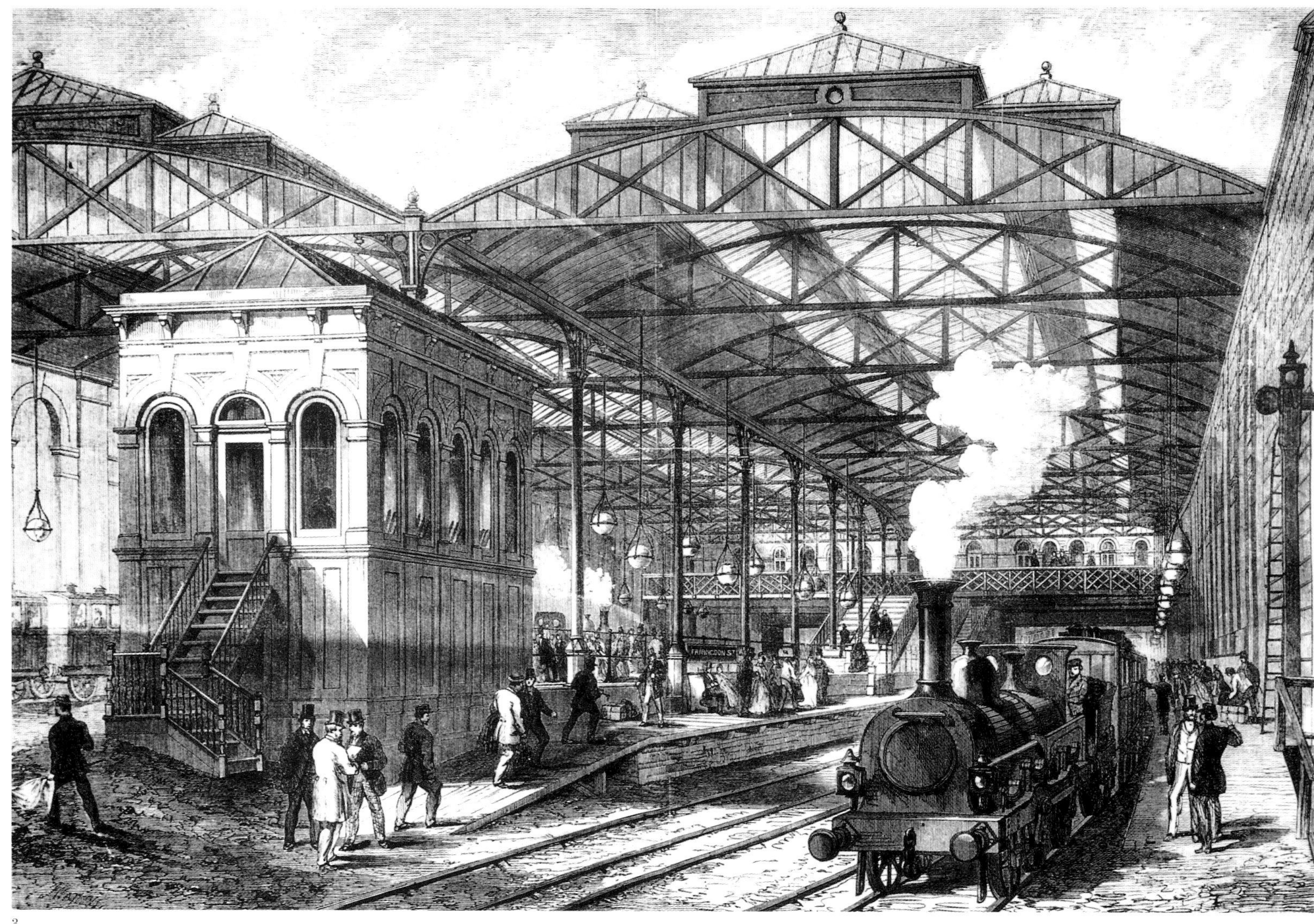

The Underground was a rough and ready service at first, without comfort or finesse. John Latrobe, an American who travelled on it in 1868, emerged "with a taste of sulphur on his lips, a weight upon his chest, a difficulty of breathing and [...] a firm determination to encounter ten jams on Ludgate Hill rather than make another trip on the Underground railway of London."[5]

William Morris, who took the line regularly to and from his home in Hammersmith, condemns it in *News from Nowhere* as a "means of travelling which civilization has forced upon us like a habit" and speaks of "that vapour-bath of hurried and discontented humanity, a carriage of the underground railway."[6]

Various devices were tried to stifle the locomotives, but travellers continued to be troubled by smoke and fumes until the cut-and-cover lines were electrified in 1905-8. The railway added to the pollution of the immediate neighbourhoods through which it passed, and depressed their economic value. The trees and bushes of Cornwall Gardens, Kensington, "were mainly black, as they were regularly covered with soot from the nearby Metropolitan Railway," remembered a resident. Grand houses nearby failed to let, owing to "considerable noise and vibrations of trains."[7] Yet the first Underground also raised the value of property around its stations, and boosted house-building in London's fashionable western suburbs. Previously the theory of British suburban railway-building had been that demand had to precede supply: the Underground turned this on its head.[8]

It is the slow, chilly, inefficient, cut-and-cover Underground that has for some reason caught the imagination of writers rather than the faster, more functional, deep-level Tube (the older Londoner still makes a distinction between the titles). The earlier lines are certainly more eventful. Here they trundle through tunnels with just the odd gap between buildings to serve as a smoke vent; there they burst out into open cuttings. Occasionally, as on the Metropolitan feeder from Edgware Road to Hammersmith, they get high up above ground and you can survey the city around you. The stations and their facilities, too, differ. The narrator of Iris Murdoch's novel, *A Word Child*, for instance, is a remorseful civil servant who wastes his days by going round the Circle and stopping for drinking sessions at the only two stations that have bars on the platforms, Sloane Square and Liverpool Street (the bars, alas, are defunct now). He muses upon "the inevitability of it all and yet its endless

4

5

6. Chalk Farm Station nearing completion, 1907.

7. L. Green's design for Oxford Circus Station, 1905. Watercolour.

6

28 variety: the awful daylight glimpses, the blessed plunges back into the dark; the stations, each unique, the sinister brightness of Charing Cross, the mysterious gloom of Regent's Park, the dereliction of Mornington Crescent, the futuristic melancholy of Moorgate, the monumental ironwork of Liverpool Street, the twining Art Nouveau of Gloucester Road, the Barbican sunk in a baroque hole, fit subject for Piranesi."[9]

Most vivid of these literary homages to the Circle Line is a famous Sherlock Holmes short story, *The Bruce-Partington Plans*. Its plot turns upon a body which is lowered from a house on to the roof of a stationary train outside Gloucester Road Station, only to fall off while going round a bend four miles further on. Everyone is baffled except the great consulting detective.[10]

After 1890 the London Underground begins to take on a new character. It burrows deep beneath the centre, thanks to electrification and ease of excavation through the clay of the metropolitan subsoil. It elaborates, intensifies, and becomes a system, albeit one at first under divided ownership and confined to districts mostly north of the Thames; and it binds the ramshackle structure of the gigantic city together through the boon of rapid travel on the "Twopenny Tube". Speed, hurry and precise time-keeping become more palpable in London life. People of modest means are able to cover greater distances to and from work and are less confined to their districts. The Methodist Church, for instance, responds by building central halls for large Sunday congregations instead of local ones for small gatherings; and the London County Council plans its sites for technical education on a city-wide basis, requir-

7

8

ing students to travel across London to them if need be. Before 1900 this would not have been possible; because London was so vast, services were mostly either localized or confined to the centre.

People could also now increasingly escape London's density and gloom to live in places like Hampstead Garden Suburb, first and most famous of many peripheral developments built in response to the Tube. Every urban railway represents finely poised centrifugal and centripetal forces. But the net effect of the near-simultaneous opening of the four original lines of the deep-level Tube (the Northern Line, 1890-1907; the Central Line, 1900; the Bakerloo Line, 1906; and the Piccadilly Line, 1906) seems to have been to usher in an epoch of urban balance and unification for London – the first stirrings of that imposition of order and of the new psychology of urban efficiency that Rasmussen was relieved to recognize.

The earliest symbols of this unifying force are the stations of the Underground Electric Railways Company of London, the so-called "Combine". Under the control of a wily American financier, C.T. Yerkes, the Combine built the Bakerloo and Piccadilly Lines, extended the Northern Line and electrified the District Line in the space of a few years (1904-7). The merits of the forty stations designed for these lines by the short-lived Leslie Green (1875-1908) have been overshadowed by the fame of later underground stations.

Green and the UERL directors grasped that the firm's stations needed a distinctive, coherent image. Being smaller in above-ground area than previous stations, they had to look both prominent and cleanly, so as to stress the non-polluting quality of electric traction. Hence the forceful, polished, oxblood-red faience of the exteriors, and the tiling throughout the walls and platforms inside. As the stations were required to pay, they were built with a mezzanine floor of lettable workshop or office space above, and framed in steel on which a heavy superstructure for offices or apartments could be added at any time. And they were kitted out with a consistent yet flexible modular vocabulary for their elevations, new to British architecture.

Leslie Green wore himself out in the work of adapting this language to the Combine's many different urban sites, often on non-rectangular street corners. Anyone who has tried to make prefabricated systems fit on irregular sites and then compares a few of these stations will recognize Green's discipline, fertility and skill. If they do not match the flamboyance of Guimard's contemporary Métro entrances in Paris, they address their more exacting brief with equal conviction. How far the UERL stations reflect American influence is a moot point. Probably the concept of the base on which a lettable superstructure could be imposed was an American one. But the urban railways that Yerkes had financed in Chicago and elsewhere were elevated lines, which (like the Paris Métro stations) did not raise the same issues of street architecture. The "kit of parts" approach to the design of railway stations and other small buildings can be found in the 19th century and was gaining ground after 1900, as companies became more image-conscious. But in no previous urban building campaign had the issues of architectural image, consistency and variation been so exhaustively addressed and solved.

Green's idiom survived him into the next generation of underground stations, such as the excellent Maida Vale (the first station to have escalators) and Kilburn Park on the Bakerloo Line extension (opened 1915). But the ideal of coherence and unity made its most powerful impact on Frank Pick (1878-1941), who was to set the design-style of the Underground between the wars. Pick was the right-hand man of Albert Stanley, Lord Ashfield (1874-1948), managing director of the UERL from 1910 and main author of the amalgamation of London's public transport system. In the British way, this came about through compromise. By buying up rival companies but accepting public obligations in exchange, Ashfield staved off the threat of municipalization and put the Combine in a position of unassailable, corporatist near-monopoly. When the London Passenger Transport Board was finally set up as a public monopoly in 1933, the policies and structure of the UERL had to be little altered. The headquarters of the new body remained those of the UERL; Ashfield continued to occupy the same boardroom and Pick's grip on the Underground image was confirmed.

It is chiefly to Pick that we owe the myth of the London Underground, the image of the coherent, patriarchal, beneficent, civic-minded system of public transport for Londoners.[11] Pick began work for the Combine in 1908, when its deep-level tubes were just opening and the financial prospects of the company looked dire. A lawyer and statistician with little background in art or design, his seminal contribution was to grasp the link between profit and presentation, so readily accepted

9. Adams, Holden and Pearson, architects, Underground Group headquarters at 55 Broadway, 1927-9, in the snow in 1931.

now, so new to Edwardian London. The American connections of the company probably had something to do with this (Ashfield had made his reputation running public transport in New Jersey). Beginning with posters as a means of selling space and getting Londoners to use the UERL's lines more between peak hours, Pick quickly educated himself into a philosophy of holistic, functional design. This he saw as the key to efficiency, popularity, unification and, beyond that, to a better climate of travel, information and culture for all of London's citizens, from distant suburbans to inveterate metropolitans.

Like many English puritans of his generation, Pick believed profoundly in the suburbs and in the countryside beyond. He had been touched by the ideas of Ebenezer Howard and wanted to get more Londoners out of the centre to its healthier and purer environs. For Pick, the persistent spread of the Underground neatly united principle and profit.

Pick found and developed his ideas through the Design and Industries Association (DIA), England's more muted equivalent to the Deutscher Werkbund. His first great success beyond the bounds of commissioning artists for Underground posters and having them well grouped on stations was the commissioning of the famous and beautiful Underground alphabet from Edward Johnston, to be used on all the company's signs and notices (1913-6). After the First World War, Pick extended his omnivorous interests into station design. About the first major group of stations, planned for the Northern Line extension to Morden, he wrote: "We are going to represent the DIA gone mad, and in order that I may go mad in good company I have got Holden to see that we do it properly."[12]

The unofficial partnership between Charles Holden (1875-1960) and Pick, lasting from about 1924 to 1939, is the classic period of London underground architecture. Holden was one of very few British architects to make the full journey from the Arts and Crafts Movement to outright European modernism. The most personal of his stations are his early ones on the extension to Morden (1924-6). They are often on corner sites like those on which Leslie Green had built. Yet they are treated quite differently, with spacious, well-lit vestibules and stripped-classical façades in dressed stone over reinforced concrete that have a hint of Loos's Vienna about them. To cheer them up, Holden makes witty use of the UERL's "bull's eye" symbol that was to become the universal logo of London Transport; it appears both in

9

colour in the clerestory windows and in the little capitals of flanking columns, to create the so-called "Underground order".

55 Broadway, the UERL headquarters built over St James's Park Station in 1928-30 and still the head office of London Regional Transport, finds Holden in ponderous mood, clothing American planning efficiency in the grey Portland stone textures he liked. It is an authoritarian building for a "dirigiste" concern. Yet it has many touches of refinement and boasts bold reliefs by Jacob Epstein, Henry Moore (his first public work), Eric Gill and others on the four façades, most of them too high up to enjoy. A touch typical of Ashfield and Pick's populist corporatism is the foundation stone, proclaiming in beautiful lettering that it was laid by the company caretaker.

In 1930 Holden and Pick visited Holland, Germany, Denmark and Sweden. They were very struck by Dudok's work in Holland, which finally freed Holden from the bonds of Edwardian gravity. The famous stations that followed during the second phase of their collaboration on the Underground, on the eastward and westward extensions of the Piccadilly Line (e.g. Osterley, Northfields, Sudbury Town, Southfields, Arnos Grove and Cockfosters), display a freshness, a calm and a consistency of detail which make them classics of modern architecture. Since most of these stations were in the open, Holden and his assistants were free from the confines of the deep tube. Lamp-posts, canopies, seats, kiosks and advertising boards are all considered

anew. Above all, the stations have a material integrity lacking in previous modernist architecture in Britain: brick goes only where brick should go, concrete looks like concrete and enjoys its own proper profiles.

Holden's firm was far from being the only one employed on the Underground by Pick, particularly after the formation of the London Passenger Transport Board in 1933. Architects, designers and artists of many kinds were set to work, in a climate of enlightened patronage. But the house-style of the Underground which evolved during the 1930s owed more to Holden than to anyone else. The relation between the in-house architects and private firms, and between the standard fittings used on all stations and the individuality of particular designs, was never simple. Design effort on the part of the LPTB encompassed not just underground stations but trains, trams, buses, trolley buses, shelters, depots, power and transformer stations and advertising. In this massive service (with 86,456 employees in 1939), the constraints of engineering efficiency and the push for integration were the determinants. Style and flair played their part, but always in subordination to a strong institutional ethic.

By the time of the Second World War, the progressive, orderly, optimistic image of the London Underground that had already struck Rasmussen in 1927 was fixed. An episode that followed, however, reminds us that sinister and creative strands continued to be bound together in Underground history. This was the invasion of the tubes by London's poorer classes for use as shelters against bombing, and the record of the shelterers made by Henry Moore – among the most profound of all artistic testaments to wartime suffering and endurance.

During the First World War, Londoners had taken to going down into the Underground to escape Zeppelin raids. The railway companies tolerated this grudgingly. In 1939 The Government and the LPTB were determined, for logistical reasons, that it would not happen again; when air raids took place, the stations were to be shut and locked for the night. Meanwhile few deep shelters had been earmarked in London; there was widespread apprehension that bombing would annihilate the city. After the first few nights of regular attack in September 1940, the East Enders took unilateral action. Some bought tickets before the raid started, rode around on trains and refused to come up; others stormed the gates at Liverpool Street. There was no way of stopping this short

10. Jacob Epstein and his sculpture
Night for 55 Broadway, 1929.

11. Aerial view of 55 Broadway,
in which the cruciform plan is evident.
At the time of opening, this was
the tallest office building in London.

of closing the Underground permanently, so the authorities had to give in. Thereafter, people were let into the stations at 4 p.m. Until the evening rush-hour was over they had to stay eight feet away from the edge of the platform; after that, four feet, until the trains stopped running and the current was turned off. They then slept wherever they could, on the platforms, the stairs or even on boards or hammocks across the tracks.[13]

This popular invasion of the London Underground has played its part in the English "myth of the Blitz" – the myth of Cockney toughness, improvisation and invincibility in the face of aerial assault. Indeed Henry Moore himself was drawn into taking part in a propaganda film of 1943, *Out of Chaos*, which celebrated the courage of the subterranean shelterers. The truth is grimmer. "They talk about those days as if they were time of a true communal spirit," wrote the playwright Bernard Kops, then a boy of twelve who was taken into the tubes. "Not to me. It was the beginning of an era of utter terror, of fear and horror."[14] Conditions in the tube shelters were appalling during the first weeks; there was no sanitation, little organization, and a spiteful attitude on the part of the authorities and middle classes. The shelterers caught impetigo, lice and scabies; bedding put up against the platform walls became infested and had to be removed; the stations stank. And yet, on being ejected in the early morning, many shelterers went straight back into a queue (where ticket touts operated) and waited all day for the afternoon, either because they had no home to go to or because they felt more secure in the Underground. 177,000 people were sheltering in this manner in late September. Organization slowly improved; new bunks, lavatories, a library service and even a food train were laid on. When the raids eased off in Spring 1941, most people left. But there were still 6,000 or more going down into the tube stations nightly when the European war ended in 1945.

Nor was the Underground safe. Twenty people died at Marble Arch when blast turned tiles on the walls into projectiles; sixty in a grisly incident at Balham, when a sewer broke in a raid and water, ballast and slime rained down on to the shelterers; 117 as a result of a direct hit at Bank in January 1941; and, worst of all, 173 suffocated at Bethnal Green in March 1943 when a false alarm caused a stampede down the station steps. The full truth about these incidents was kept from Londoners.

Such was the world which Henry Moore depicted in his shelter drawings – not as an official war-artist, but as one of many people touched, when returning by tube to his own comfortable home, by the eerie, nightly spectacle of the shelterers. He likened it to "the hold of a slave-ship on its way from Africa to America, full of hundreds and hundreds of people who were having things done to them that they were quite powerless to resist [...] I saw people lying on the platforms at all the stations we stopped at [...] I had never seen so many reclining figures and even the train tunnels seemed to be like the holes in my sculpture."[15]

For some weeks Moore roamed all over the station shelters, concentrating much of his time on an unfinished tube tunnel between Liverpool Street and Bethnal Green where sleepers lay all along the tracks. During these visits he made notes on the back of an envelope but never sketched. "Odoriferous slum dwellers, frightened small businessmen these cannot be: they are an image of Humanity itself, in heroic repose," says Angus Calder of Moore's magnificent, sombre drawings.[16] In the same way, they can stand as a monument to the Underground's long list of anonymous heroes and victims, from the Thames Tunnel to the King's Cross fire disaster of 1987, when 31 people died.

What of the London Underground today? For almost forty years after 1945 the system rested on its laurels, sure of its monopoly position and of the pre-eminent role it played in the psychology and shape of Greater London. When underground extension began again after a twenty-year gap with the Victoria Line (opened 1968-71) and the first phase of the Jubilee Line (1977), the Pick formula linking design with operation still carried conviction, albeit with less commercial logic. There then followed a period of bad management, low investment and political inconsistency, coming to a climax after 1986. Sorely needed but ill-coordinated modernization programmes wrecked the integrity of many stations. Even the Johnston alphabet was in part wantonly abandoned, though the posters always stayed up to standard. Trains became less frequent, more prone to breakdown, more dangerous late at night, more crowded in the centre. Fares rose to levels above those of almost all other cities with underground systems, despite the challenge and pollution of the car. In many of those other cities fresh subway systems proliferated, learning from and surpassing London's example.

12. Interior of Hammersmith and City
Line carriage, showing upholstery, 1937.

13. Adams, Holden and Pearson,
architects, Sudbury Town Station,
booking hall, 1931.

14. Grouping of advertising posters
at Manor House Station, 1935.

32   Things are a little better now. There is faith not so much in the integrity of the network as in the absolute necessity for maintaining and updating the whole of London's railway network, of which the Underground only ever controlled a part. The building of the Docklands Light Railway showed faith, of a cheeseparing kind, in this goal. After many delays the Jubilee Line extension is in progress; its stations are being designed or refurbished with an indiscipline of which Pick would not have approved, but by stylish architects. If they lack the homogeneity of the classic era of Underground design, that is because London has shifted once again.

Today it is a more fragmented, robust and individualistic place than the London that Green or Pick or Holden conceived: youthful, raw at the centre, uneven at the edges, yet on the whole far more pleasant than the fringes of most cities of its size. We partly have Pick and his colleagues to thank for that. In retrospect, their achievement was more elegant than permanent. The lasting homogenization and order they sought were too ambitious to achieve. Perhaps they were always papering over cracks; perhaps too the golden age of the London Underground, like most golden ages, was never quite so golden. Yet for most of this century it has managed to deliver pride, definition and shape to a great world city.

1. Steen Eiler Rasmussen, "First Impressions of London," translated in *AA Files*, No. 20, Autumn 1990, pp. 15-21. The original German version appeared in *Wasmuths Monatshefte für Baukunst*, No. 12, 1928, pp. 304-13.
2. Francis Way, *A Frenchman Sees England in the Fifties*, 1935, pp. 107-8. See also Alison Lockwood, *Passionate Pilgrims*, 1981, p. 181.
3. Jan and Cora Gordon, *The London Roundabout*, 1933, p. 106.
4. A. Lockwood, *op. cit.*, p. 397.
5. Ibid., pp. 395-6.
6. William Morris, *Selected Writings and Designs*, 1962, p. 183.
7. "Southern Kensington: Kensington Square to Earl's Court," *Survey of London*, vol. 42, 1986, pp. 156, 402.
8. See *Railway Times*, 2 February 1878, quoted in *Survey of London*, op. cit., p. 401.
9. Iris Murdoch, *A Word Child* (London: Penguin Edition, 1976), p. 38.
10. Sir Arthur Conan Doyle, *Sherlock Holmes. The Complete Short Stories*, 1928 edition, pp. 968-99.
11. For Pick see the excellent biography by Christian Barman, *The Man Who Built London Transport*, 1979.
12. Ibid., p. 118.

12

13

14

15. Adams, Holden and Pearson,
architects, Arnos Grove Station, 1938.

15

13. For this episode see especially Angus Calder,
The People's War, 1969, and *The Myth of the Blitz*,
1991; Norman Longmate, *How We Lived Then*,
1971; Tom Harrisson, *Living Through the Blitz*,
1976; Joanna Mack and Steven Humphries, *The
Making of Modern London 1939-1945: London at
War*, 1985; and Philip Ziegler, *London at War*, 1995.
14. Bernard Kops, *The World is a Wedding*, 1963,
p. 68.
15. Richard Trench and Ellis Hillman, *London under London*, 1984, p. 21.
16. A. Calder, *The Myth of the Blitz* cit., p. 143.

1-4. Tile designs in some of Leslie
Green's stations: South Kensington,
Covent Garden, Camden Town, Holborn.
© David Lawrence.

5-8. Tile designs by Alan Fletcher at 4
of the 12 original Victoria Line stations,
1968-72: Victoria, Highbury & Islington,
Green Park, Warren Street.

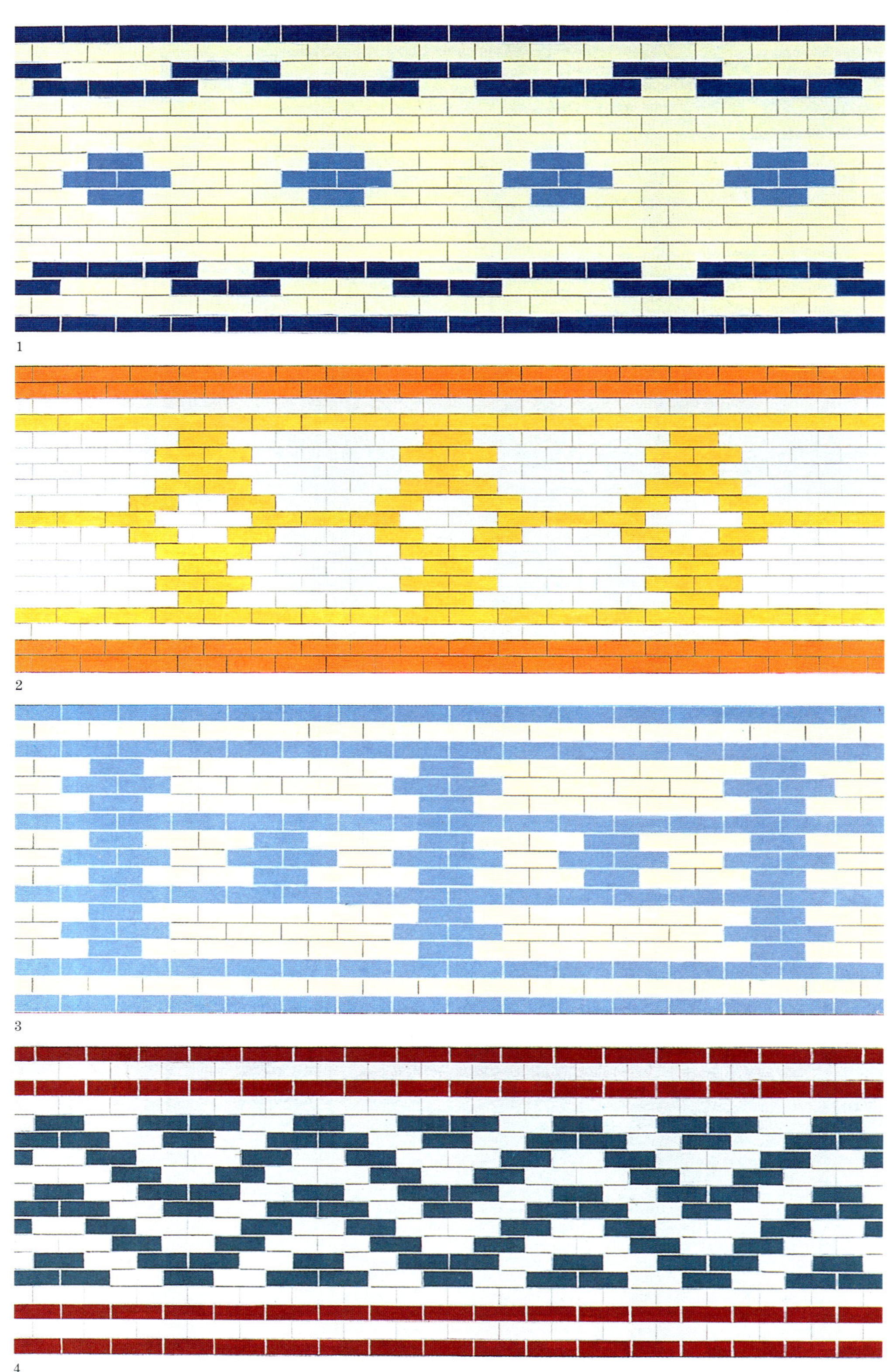

An Underground Memoir

Bond Street

I joined London Transport Architect's Department in 1977 as a temporary architectural assistant to the team completing the fitting out of the Jubilee Line. Under construction since 1972 it was a £90 million engineering led project, and it was clear that the engineers saw us, the architects, as the small birds that housekeep the back of a rhinoceros. I was allocated the task of designing the waterproof lining for a newly excavated transformer chamber at Bond Street.

The size of St Mark's church in North Audley Street above, yet invisible to the public, this proto-crypt was persistently leaking through its immense and nominally waterproof secant piles, threatening the high voltage equipment within. Our job was to capture the flow into secret gutters behind brick lining walls and conduit it safely to the ubiquitous pumps that keep the Underground dry. No one was looking, this was architects without architecture,[1] tidying up after the civil engineers had finished their gargantuan excavations.

It soon became clear why a significant number of the architectural staff had backgrounds in the design of oil and chemical plants for there were no "external elevations" on the drawing boards, just massive layouts peppered with references to standard details. The axonometrics of the underground stations were, in pre-CAD days, works of art. Indeed I was advised to remember that the fundamental design principle was hydraulic – and to keep the involuntary passengers flowing in and out of the system without blockages or turbulence. The Underground has a notoriously tightly restricted layout, with every inch at a premium.[2]

For the architects the design ethos was dominated by routines and constraints set by the railway operating and electrical engineers. The master clock in Holden's Broadway headquarters, synchronising the 273 station clocks throughout the system, was emblematic of a necessarily autocratic railway culture.

This was another world for a former student from the anti-authoritarian 1960s who had never seen military service nor worked for the state.

Of course there were compensations for being an "invisible architect". Not least a travel pass for all LT buses and trains. As a suburban boy I had pilgrimaged to the metropolis via Holden's south London temples. Now I became an initiate into a guild of those with free movement within the public domain and privileged access to its backstage. I found myself climbing the spiral stairs of ventilation towers pulsating with the hot breath of the trains far below, to emerge high above street level, or looking from the darkened interior of the pressure relief shafts through massive louvres at the passengers pressing past oblivious. This was a shadow city of blackened cast iron tunnels, lit by low wattage bulbs, beyond the reach of the general public. Become a member of the cast of Lang's *Metropolis*, I was touched by a perverse romance – a stage hand observing the cast of thousands from the wings.[3]

It seemed that we were expected not simply to assist the nervous public's safe passage but in some way to shield them from the muscular and claustrophobic tensions of this immense interior world. Heroically taming the intestinal profiles with smooth floors, vertical walls and deceptive laminated ceilings, an il-

lusion fixed by uniform fluorescent light, to hold their panic at bay.

Yet the era of Holden and Pick's magisterial and co-ordinated pre-war design seemed deeply remote, although echoes reverberated through the standard details, Johnston's ubiquitous Sans-Serif and the sheer weight of the historic achievement, still the largest underground railway in the world. However, passenger usage had been steadily falling, decades of under-investment having taken their toll in fabric and service, the post-war system was perceived at best as dull, at worst run down and dangerous.[4]

The exception was the only line built since the war, the Victoria, completed in 1969. Designed with considerable restraint and attention to detail, this work struck me then and now as admirable, composed in muted greys with stainless steel and brushed aluminium, with its quirky seat back tiles, with their cryptic allusions to life on the surface – a maze for Warren Street – added to give "a touch of humanity to the rather severe platforms."[5] The philosophy of the Design Panel responsible, including the pivotal post-war designer Misha Black, was well expressed by their comment that "the stations may be criticised for appearing visually unexciting but we consider that preferable to a transient popularity without lasting qualities."[6] This was the patrician design language of the Design Council, the post-war modernist establishment, committed to a widening democratic rationality, holding rampant commercialism at bay armed with judicious state funding.

Shaken in the 1960s, in the 1970s this confidence in the post-war consensus collapsed.

5

6

7

8

9, 10. Charing Cross ticket hall, 1979.

9

36

10

And with it went the design values of civility and coherence imposed from above. In the Department the growing notion that the stations had to "sell themselves" to attract passengers coincided with a populist graphic iconoclasm which rejected the muted, controlled and recessive aesthetic for "variety". The architecture of the Jubilee Line exhibited the growing tensions of this new pluralism and incoherence.

Charing Cross

Having served my apprenticeship in the private depths of Bond Street I moved early in 1978 to the shallower world of public subways at Charing Cross Station. Here a new Underground ticket hall had been excavated in the forecourt of the railway terminus, immediately beneath the famous medieval cross from which all London mileages are measured. The massive ticket hall excavations included reinforced subway arms worming their way to four new surface exits as well as connecting to the existing 19th century station and Coutt's bank across the Strand. Structures that were essentially utilitarian engineering awaiting their architectural "cladding". As sub-surface pedestrian streets they were also clearly a significant addition to the public realm at the very centre of the city. Of this there was no discussion nor as a public utility was any public consultation required.

Twisted by obstructions, services, surface loads, the subways had no consistent geometry, with floors, walls and ceilings all varying in alignment and pitch. Yet they were redeemed by an accidentally grand space formed between the basement flanks of the old station and the boundary of the new ticket hall. My task was to line the raw concrete to provide water channels, service routes and a durable surface. As a 24-hour subway vandal resistance was considered the guiding virtue, my palette was severely limited to tile, cement, stone and steel.

Rejecting static pattern making, even the incorporation of I-Ching hexagrams, as gratuitous compared to the fundamental drama of penetrating the ground I set an unvarying horizontal colour banding throughout the entrances and passageways. This deepened in tone as the low subway tunnels descended, only to reveal its full spectrum in the vaulting antechamber. Intended to relieve the disorientation caused by the engineered profiles, providing each person with Ariadne's thread to the labyrinth, the strata mastered the apertures that punctuated the passage walls and even formed the columns like beachside souvenirs. I now appreciate I was echoing the earliest station tiling designs that had over the years been submerged by advertisements.[7] The stratified subways literally wrapped round the new ticket hall chamber, the territory of London Transport proper, and here a very different design approach prevailed, which I witnessed but had no part in. From here on, Ariadne could offer no help.

In the ticket hall you could say that the 1960s had finally made it Underground, evicting the paternal designers with their good manners and anonymity. The LT architects used a visual language dominated by the relentless articulation of elements and bizarrely glossy surfaces. Sharing a sub-text of rebellion against deference to commercial advertising – "why should they have all the fun?" – and inspired by the radical designers of Milan, by Sottsass, by Olivetti and the sexy world of film and product design, the architects launched a GRP cladding "kit-of-parts".[8]

Ignoring the lofty structural cavern, a low suspended slatted ceiling with parallel bands of strip lighting hung across the flow of passengers, dissolving and confusing the ceiling plane – like running a cheese grater though your hair. Ahead, the lurid green ticket offices, chemical blue column cladding and emergency yellow ticket barrier boxes all screamed for attention in their new shiny GRP suits, set against a dark background and floated from the floor by black rubber negative skirtings. Studded rubber flooring suddenly changing the conventional surface of public life into a deadened resilience. Here was the language of boutiques and Starship *Enterprise*. The ascending passengers eager to reach the surface world, each Persephone rising inexorably from the troubled underworld, were met not by harbingers of day but garish booths jostling for attention like bouncers in an involuntary night club. The ticket hall's inversion of proprieties, this loss of control, not merely of colour, texture and form, but also in its deep confusion as to an appropriate public psychology, authentically announced the ponderous bonhomie of post-modernism.

Much more successful was a series of massive platform length murals in the refurbished tunnels below. David Gentleman's enlarged medieval wood blocks reproduced onto a white laminate panel, carefully integrating the signage and furniture, had the effect of dramatically widening the perceived platform space.

13

13. Paddington Bakerloo Line platform.

14. Eduardo Paolozzi, study for the mosaic at the Oxford Street entrance to Tottenham Court Road Station, 1984. Watercolour.

15. Eduardo Paolozzi, Tottenham Court Road Central Line murals, 1984.

38

14

15

On the Jubilee Line seat backs, rendered as illuminated windows, he wittily revealed a prospect of Trafalgar Square above, like a camera obscura. Surreal enlargements of paintings, including Botticelli's *Venus and Mars* from the National Gallery above, introduced a startling intimacy to the suddenly child-like passengers.

The subways were opened with the Jubilee Line in the summer of 1979, serving for a glorious afternoon as a buffet for the opening celebrations. I left to work above ground again, blinking in the daylight, glad to be invited to design houses on a hillside in Milton Keynes with elevations, weather and trees.

Postscript

In the spate of station improvements that followed the opening of the Jubilee Line in 1979, the enthusiasm for loose and panelled elements declined but not the appetite for garish graphics. Reverting to tiling, London Transport commissioned a mixed batch of designs for a number of central stations, notably the misguided attempt by Eduardo Paolozzi to "bring the fast-moving world above ground down to meet the arriving passengers"[9] at Tottenham

16, 17. Mac Cormac Jamieson Prichard, Southwark Station on the Jubilee Line extension presently under construction, showing the ticket hall and the intermediate concourse.

Court Road. All too often the ironic layering of confusion upon anxiety as a sign of "variety" nicely expressed post-modernism's special gift to the public realm. In a number of stations obtrusive and visually confusing patterning was enthusiastically scattered across the tunnel platform walls and passage surfaces, further heightening the information load of passengers to intolerable limits.

Most successful were those schemes that referred to the excavated space, acknowledging rather than concealing its chthonic nature. At Holborn archaeological fragments from the British Museum lined the platform wall for the passengers to excavate in imagination.

At Baker Street the original brick vaulting was exposed, lit and celebrated while at Paddington fragments of Marc Brunel's tunnelling machines are printed on the tiles.

The careful refurbishment and public re-appreciation of Holden's work at Piccadilly also signalled a shift towards conserving the best fabric of the system.

These initiatives were hampered by episodic funding, and have been criticised for being cosmetic while basic infrastructure such as primitive signalling was left unmodernised.

In November 1987 an ancient timber escalator ignited and a fireball engulfed the ticket hall at King's Cross, its ferocity assisted by paint finishes, timber and a suspended ceiling. This traumatic fire killed 31 people and injured many others, drawing bitter attention to the lack of investment in the safety of the system and, incidentally, to the unconsidered use of materials. As a result stone, cast masonry, ceramics, exposed metal and vitreous enamel have displaced the "Pick 'n Mix" of plastics, rubber, GRP and laminated sheet to the greater benefit and integrity of new designs.

By 1990 London Transport had re-stabilised their Design Strategy, encouraging greater simplicity and sobriety explicitly "to create a calming visual environment of neutral colours and rationalised signage." They also commissioned a number of independent consultants, including Foster and MacCormac among others, to design stations including those for the Jubilee Line extension now under construction, designs generally characterised by bold structural expression, solid construction and the admission of daylight wherever possible.

If the post-modernist binge is dissipating and salutary architectural lessons appear to have been learnt, the commercial pressures to maximise revenue continue to challenge the fragile coherence of this remarkable system.

17

Proposals to sell off the 11 lines as separate enterprises and dispense with government investment may well result in the operators decorating their trains in distinct "attractive" liveries. Already London Underground are running an experimental train painted all over with advertising.[10] Above ground the vaunted red bus fleet has become a chaotic mix of colours and types under multiple franchises. Below ground, it is a good question whether the tangible and intangible civic values of coherence and continuity built up in the past sixty years will continue without the sustained investment of public funds within an integrated transport policy for the city itself.

1. Scarcely Rudowsky's seminal *Architecture without Architects* that had so inspired me as a student.
2. "The whole thing was built with vision but little forethought, the holes are too small." Denis Tunnicliffe, Managing Director of London Underground Ltd. Interview *Independent* on Sunday, 22nd October 1995.
3. Ellis Hillman and Richard Trench's *London under London*, 1985, marvellously illustrates the complexity of this world. I would like to dedicate this article to Ellis Hillman who died 21st January 1996, and clearly found wicked inspiration in the subterranean city.
4. *Changing Stations – a review of London Underground design 1980-1993* (London Underground Ltd. Architectural Services, 1993), p. 7.

5. P. 197 in David Lawrence's excellent popular history *Underground Architecture* Note (London: Pub. Capital Transport, 1994).
6. Ibid., p. 168.
7. Ibid., p. 35.
8. Known on site by those who had to assemble the intolerable tolerances, and the endless "specials", as the "pit of farts".
9. Lawrence, *op. cit.*, p. 177.
10. *Evening Standard*, 1st February 1996.

Interchanges

Introduction. Definition

40 The great majority of the 270 stations served by London Underground could be described as interchanges because buses pass nearly all of them and there is, at least, *potential* for transferring between bus and Underground. This definition would be too broad for our purposes

The Tube Map incorporates the small ring symbol at only 56 of the stations common to two or more of the lines or branches shown on the map (the Underground lines, the Docklands Light Railway and a few sections of the Railtrack network) and treats interchange with lines/modes not shown differently. This definition is too narrow for our purposes.

Instead, all the locations at which Underground passengers choose to transfer between lines or branches or between public transport modes in significant numbers are considered to be interchanges. In London, the other modes are now bus, coach, air transport, light rail and those rail services (suburban, main line and international) operated by British Rail, its subsidiaries and their successors.

Research into passenger behaviour suggests a strong reluctance to interchange but public transport users *have* to transfer (at least once) if there is no direct vehicle between the origin and destination of their journey. Some may *choose* to interchange additionally if they save a significant amount of time and/or money by doing so or they achieve another personal objective, such as greater comfort or a retail transaction. This review looks at why, where and how passengers transfer and at interchange design.

The Network

The Tube Map shows that each Underground line has at least one station in common *with nearly every other major Underground line* (i.e. discounting the short East London and Waterloo & City Lines). The District Line currently has no station in common with the Jubilee Line: these lines will have two interchanges when the Jubilee Line Extension is completed. The District and Metropolitan Lines have no station in common either, but other lines provide direct services between some of their respective stations.

By contrast, the District and Circle Lines have 18 stations in common: passengers travelling from some Circle Line origins to some District Line destinations (or vice versa) therefore have a large choice of where to transfer

1

(this is complicated by the District Line's various branches). There are many other Underground journeys for which the passenger has a choice of interchanges.

Passenger Information

Where there is a choice of interchange, the passenger's decision can be influenced by the information presented. The Tube Map, in how it represents interchanges, distances and lines diagrammatically, the Travelcard zones map and some of the information on trains and within stations all suggest where to interchange. If the information relates to a specific train timetable, the advice may have to change when the timetable changes. The very naming of stations and lines can influence the choice of interchange and make it easier for those unfamiliar with the network.

The Hammersmith & City Line was built and at times managed as a branch of the Metropolitan Line. It used to be represented by the same colour on maps: the old name is featured in some of the old photographs. Giving the Hammersmith & City its own name and colour in publicity material and on the map made it easier for passengers to find the right platform at interchange locations such as Baker Street which had six Metropolitan Line platforms.

Capacity

London Transport aims to attract new passengers onto public transport but overcrowding occurs on some sections of London's Rail network during peaks. One benefit of any choice between interchanges is that it provides scope for encouraging passengers to use those trains and interchanges which have spare capacity and to avoid overcrowding others. An alternative route can also help passengers at times of service disruption.

All significant proposed changes to the provision of public transport in London are now tested for various criteria by means of computer models. The RAILPLAN model is outlined in *Appraising Public Transport Network Options for London*. Another model, described in *Pedroute. Modelling Pedestrian Congestion. A Design and Safety Aid* is used for improving conditions in existing congested stations, optimising the design of new stations and assessing the safety of stations and developing appropriate safety criteria. *Pedroute* aims to overcome potential problems at stairwells, exits, entrances, escalators, lifts and concourses.

When new lines/interchanges are planned (e.g. the Jubilee Line Extension now being

2

built), the computer models ensure that the substantial costs of new construction beneath London are related to accurate forecasts of usage, so as to avoid under- or over-provision of capacity.

Some computer models of the network quantify changes in *perceived passenger journey times*: this includes the amount of time taken to get from one line or mode to another (by walking/lift/escalator/moving walkway) at any interchange, how long the passenger is likely to have to wait before boarding the vehicle on the next part of his/her journey: this depends on the train timetable. Less comfortable elements of the journey (walking, waiting on a platform, travelling on an overcrowded train) are "weighted" more heavily. Where the proposed significant change is predicted to cause many passengers to reroute, the likely change in patronage of the relevant interchanges can be quantified.

At Victoria, the interchange route between the subsurface and tube Underground lines, used by 18 million passengers in 1995, previously incorporated two escalators (one up, one down) and a fixed staircase arranged in parallel. Additional peak interchange capacity is being created, inter alia, by *replacing* the fixed staircase with an additional peak-direction escalator. This creates an obstacle for passengers unable to use *moving* escalators, including those accompanied by dogs (e.g. some blind passengers) which are excluded to avoid serious paw injuries. The solutions adopted are: (i) a means for disabled passengers to call for staff assistance and (ii) for the third escalator to be switched off outside peak hours so that it can then be used as a fixed staircase.

When there were only a few, short underground lines in London, there was only a limited need for interchange between underground lines. In fact the "Inner Circle" [the reason for this old name is explained in Gordon Hafter's paper] provided a direct train service between many of the original Metropolitan Railway Company stations and the original Metropolitan District Railway Company stations.

The early additions to the network involved constructing branches or adding loops to existing lines. These enabled many new *direct* services to be introduced rapidly, with trains tending to share the same sections of track in the central area.

There was also comparatively little need for *interchange between underground and main lines* because the original underground lines were built as extensions of various main lines, to similar technical standards, and trains were able to operate directly between both systems. This required track connections ("junctions"). As London's rail network was extended, station infrastructure was rebuilt, demand evolved and technology changed, some of the connections were severed and new ones were created.

The general separation of the underground system at main line termini, introduction of new underground lines in the central area and new main line termini, caused these termini, including the case studies of Euston and Liverpool Street, to become important Underground interchanges. Nowadays around 40% of the 400,000 passengers arriving at the Central London main line stations in the morning peak complete their journeys by Underground.

The original underground lines were built on the "cut and cover" principle, an average 7.3 metres below ground level. Most of those built since the 1890s are "tube" lines and an average 24.4 metres below ground level.

At the many interchanges between the tube and surface or subsurface lines, considerable vertical separation has to be overcome.

Many of the tube lines were originally built with lifts to/from the surface and, in some cases, these were also used by interchanging passengers. In general, a policy was pursued since the 1920s of *replacing* lifts with escalators where the growth of traffic justified the substantial engineering costs: escalators have a much higher hourly passenger capacity, they

3. Luminous panel at Euston Station advising that the first train is for Archway and that "When no through train is shown change at Archway for Mill Hill East & Barnet Branches," 1968. This advice made Archway a de facto interchange.

4. Metropolitan circulating area at Baker Street, showing retail units and postboxes inside barrier and arrows to "Metropolitan Line", 1969.

3

4

are less problematic than lifts when they stop working and they are available instantly to passengers compared with the possible need to wait for a lift-car.

There are now 301 escalators but only 66 lifts at Underground stations. At Gloucester Road and Shadwell, lifts are used by interchanging passengers. There are moving walkways used by interchanging passengers at Bank and at our case study of Heathrow Terminals 1, 2, 3.

In connection with London Transport's newer legal obligations and policies towards disabled passengers, lifts are being introduced or reintroduced at selected locations so as to provide "step-free access" for those unable to use the adjacent escalators.

The first modern installation of a lift now used for this purpose was at Heathrow Central (renamed Heathrow Terminals 1, 2 and 3), subsequently at several of the other case study stations. Bank/Monument is another example: a lift for mobility-impaired passengers was constructed when the fully-accessible Docklands Light Railway was extended to this Underground station. The Jubilee Line Extension will bring more escalators, lifts and (at Waterloo) moving walkways.

Interchange stations tended to experience particular growth when the lines they served were extended into the suburbs before and after the Second World War. In spite of the name of the company, most of London Underground's route-mileage and most of its stations are now *above* ground. Most of the interchanges (including many of the 56 defined on the Tube Map), however, are *literally* underground being within or near the Circle Line, which circumscribes the busy heart of the network: the London rail network is now characterised by having strong radial routes but, apart from the North London Line and aforementioned Circle Line, comparatively few orbital routes.

Current Strategy

One element of London Transport Planning Strategy is to develop new orbital routes, not necessarily operated by London Underground, with appropriate interchanges so as: (i) to attract onto public transport journeys which are currently made by private car; (ii) to relieve overcrowding on some of the radial rail routes and some of the Central Area interchanges, by providing an alternative for passengers now travelling into the Central Area and back out again on another line.

Examples of orbital rail links are parts of the Jubilee Line Extension, now under construction, and the proposed northern extension to the East London Line.

A consequence of all the earlier additions to the network is that the Metropolitan Line, the District Line, the Circle Line, the Hammersmith & City Line, components of the Northern Line (a merger of the first deep-level tube and other lines), the Piccadilly Line (especially as it was between 1933 and 1964) and the Bakerloo Line (especially as it was between 1939 and 1979) all share tracks with other services. These lines feature or featured trunk sections, branches and loops. Some of the stations and some of the complex junctions (where branches or loops leave the trunk section) are closely-spaced, especially in the Central Area.

Recent tendency has been for Underground lines, including the Victoria Line opened in stages 1968-72, to be built as (or converted to) operationally simpler lines, with few or no branches or junctions, and stations spaced more widely apart.

The Victoria Line provides higher speed, greater hourly capacity, simpler operations and passenger information but does not serve as many stations *directly* as a typical older line with branches. On the other hand, 15 of the 16 stations now served by the Victoria Line are interchanges with other rail services. 5 of these interchanges are "same level".

Oxford Circus saw 28 million passengers changing between Underground lines during 1995 making it the busiest station from that point of view; passengers entering/leaving the system and interchanging to/from buses there were *additional*. Victoria Underground station was busiest in terms of *total usage*: many passengers interchange between Underground and main line trains, including services to/from Gatwick Airport.

The Jubilee Line first opened in 1979 and incorporated what had been the Stanmore Branch of the Bakerloo Line with new tunnels south of Baker Street. Some journeys which had previously required an interchange could

5. Pedroute output for Bond Street
CrossRail Station.

6. Pedroute output for Liverpool Street/
Moorgate CrossRail Station.

now be made directly. Other journeys which had previously been available directly now required an interchange and some journeys continued to require an interchange but at a different location. Bond Street station was intended, amongst other things, to relieve overcrowding at Oxford Circus.

The Jubilee Line Extension will add 10 stations to that line of which 9 will be interchanges; more lines, especially those like the Victoria and Jubilee Lines, mean many more interchange stations.

Where new lines provide a faster and/or more direct route, they can help reduce pressure on the old interchanges on parallel routes.

The Impact of Fares and Fare Collection Policies Upon Interchange Usage. Fares Policy

Rail passengers in London have generally always had a choice between buying single tickets (for one journey), return tickets (for two journeys on the same day) and period tickets (which allow an unlimited number of journeys during a day/week/month/year). There used to be very few period bus tickets.

Historically, tickets tended to restrict each passenger to a specific mode or modes (bus, Underground, British Rail) and rail tickets to any "reasonable" route. Fares were related to distance via the shortest route. For some journeys, the Circle Line was so circuitous (but often easier for those with mobility impairments) that a higher fare was charged. To avoid this higher fare, the passenger would have to travel via one of the tube routes across the central area and use any relevant interchange(s).

In general, varying the route and/or mode would often cause the passenger to have to make a significant additional payment.

In the 1980s, the route restrictions were relaxed and a zonal fare system (covering all major modes) evolved, which now gives passengers hoping to avoid additional payment much more flexibility about which route they may take on the journey and which mode(s) of transport they use. In particular the Travelcard, which gives the right to make unlimited journeys on all lines and all modes within defined zones and time periods, has become extremely popular with passengers.

The Travelcard has caused more use of public transport and much more use of interchange in London: nowadays it is easier and cheaper for passengers to vary their modes, routes and interchanges according to personal preferences.

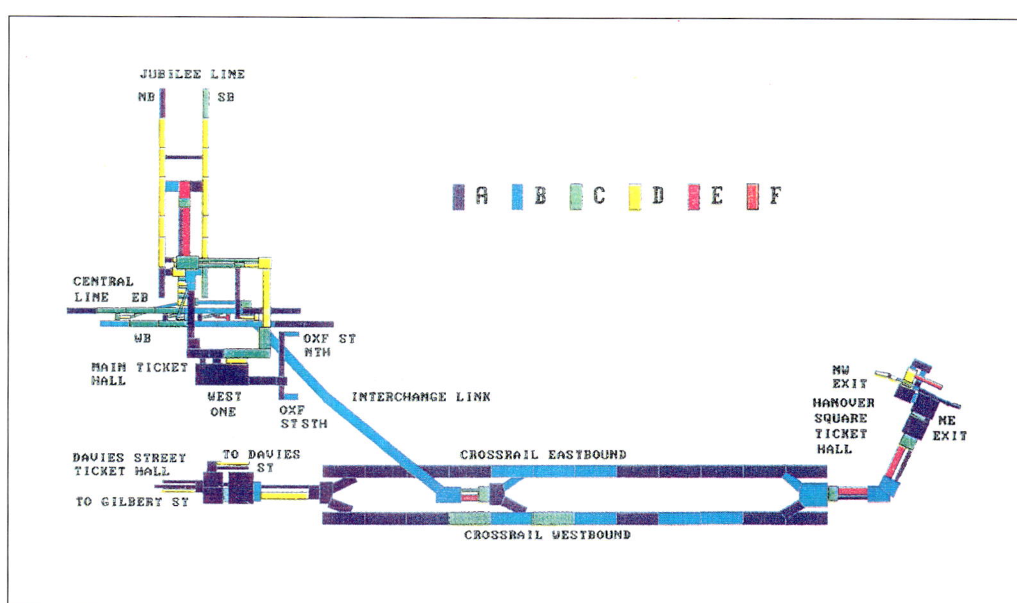

5

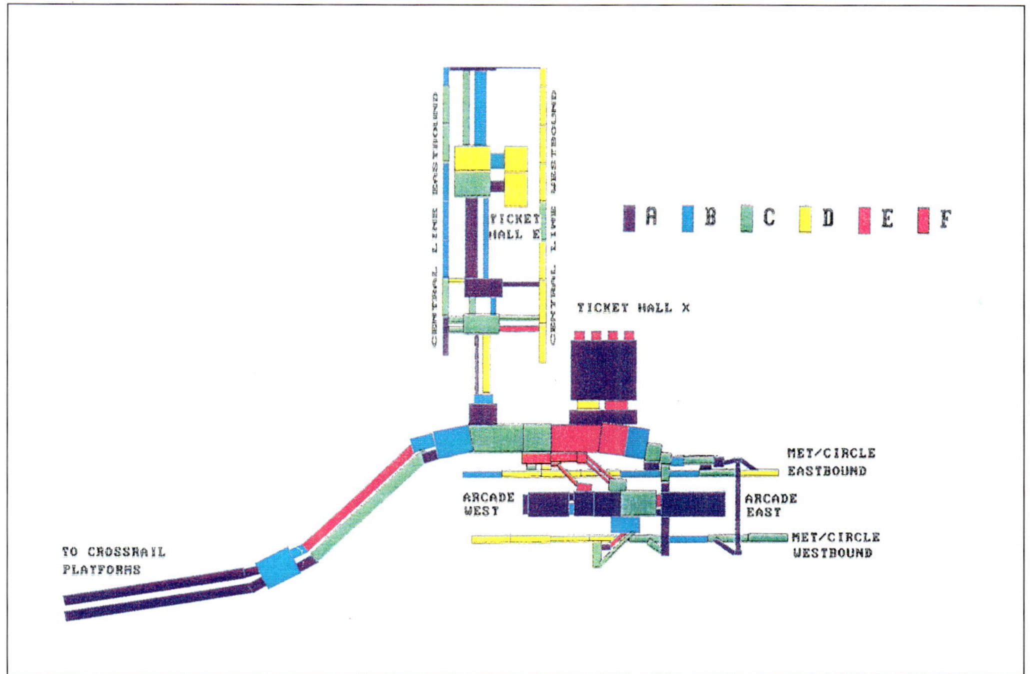

6

7. Euston escalator.
Photo Ian Bell.

7

8. Poster image describing improved interchange arrangements at South Kensington, 1973.

44 *Fare Collection Policy*

The selling and checking of tickets has become much more automated. This and security considerations have caused many ticket offices and ticket machines to be rebuilt into the wall of ticket halls (instead of the middle) and for automatic ticket-checking gates to replace the staffed cubicles, especially within Travelcard zone 1 which contains many of the important Underground interchanges. It was an enormous challenge to redesign and rebuild the old ticket halls so as accommodate the additional space and different functional requirements of the new electronic equipment and magnetically-encoded tickets. The impact on retail units was very profound.

At certain locations, a large new ticket hall replaced two or more smaller ticket halls.

Where the design of the interchange station now requires the passenger to exit through one automatic barrier and re-enter through another ("Out of station" interchange as explained later), it is essential that the exit barriers are programmed to give back the ticket to the passenger for this purpose. Some passengers, who have in fact finished their journey, are surprised to receive back a ticket which has theoretical onward validity!

Magnetically-encoded tickets and the automatic barriers that read them create certain ergonomic problems, especially if the passenger is carrying heavy luggage. Some interchanges, especially those at main line termini, became slightly more onerous when automatic barriers were installed. Other interchanges became slightly easier with the removal of intermediate staffed barriers (e.g. at Paddington if changing between Bakerloo and District/Circle Lines).

As well as ticket-checking, the automatic gates are capable of providing large amounts of data about when and where passengers travel. This important management information is difficult and expensive to obtain accurately by other means. Smartcards would appear to overcome some of the ergonomic problems associated with magnetically-encoded tickets and can provide even more data about travel patterns. Smartcard trials have been undertaken in London.

The Evolution of Retailing at Interchanges. Avoiding "The Wrong Kind of Mastic"

The great cost of providing and maintaining space below the ground in London means that retail units tend to be small in area, compared to those above ground. However the number

8

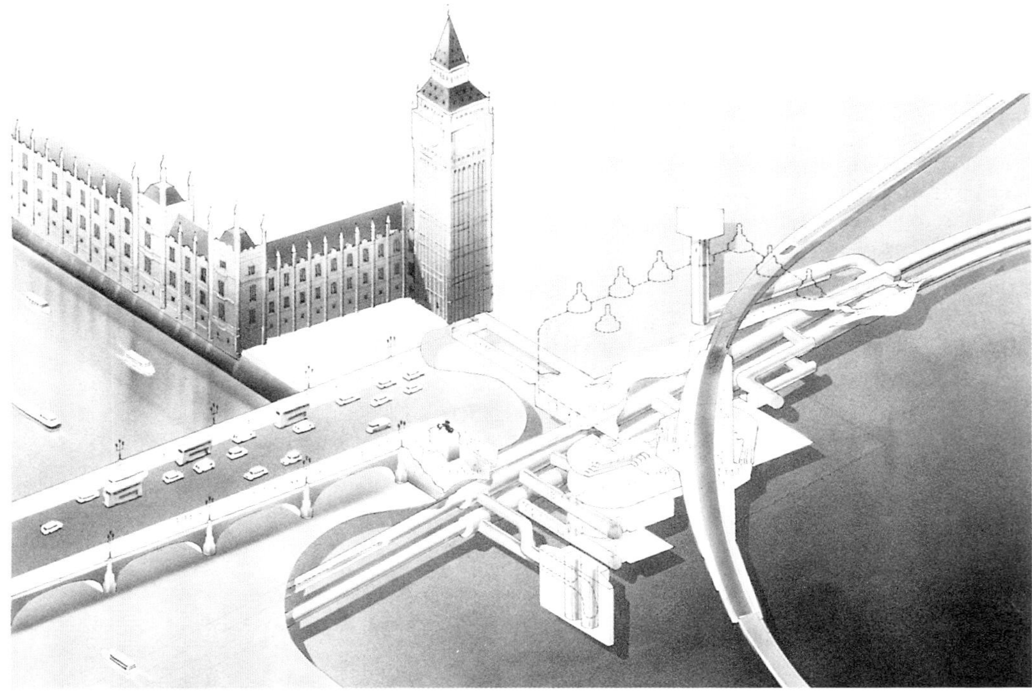

9

of potential customers passing by can be very large indeed. For example, 84 million passengers (equivalent to the whole population of Germany) used Victoria Underground station in 1995: paradoxically more retail sales take place there outside the commuting peaks when the station is less overcrowded.

Subject to the overriding requirements of operational safety, London Transport aims to maximise the rental from tenancies on its property, including Underground interchange stations. The rental agreements are therefore based on a percentage of annual turnover (subject to a minimum figure) and tenants are carefully targeted and competitive bids sought so to maximise turnover per square metre available: market leaders are preferred and tenants encouraged to refit the premises regularly. "Gap analysis" investigates which retailing needs are not currently being served at the location concerned. The introduction of telephones on station platforms (which share the ordinary platform electrical power supply) and sales of telephone cards (from adjacent chocolate machines), have been one success story. Another is the installation, over the last year, of automatic cash machines at stations; agreements have so far been reached with three major banks and a building society, which are closing some of their High Street branches.

As well as the analysis undertaken for operational and safety requirements (which have tended to increase), the precise routing and socio-economic grouping of passengers through each station complex is the subject of commercial scrutiny. The retail units sometimes have to be situated away from the main passenger flows and any situation which could cause retail customers to linger, and perhaps exacerbate station overcrowding, must be avoided.

Land Use Issues

Developments well-served by public transport are more likely to encourage people to use public transport than those located remote from e.g. an Underground station. This is why London Transport encourages appropriate development close to stations and accepts relevant commercial advertising.

The West One shopping development above Bond Street station, described in the case studies at the end of this article, is an example of a shopping complex where the retail area is not owned by London Transport. Interchange stations, by virtue of being located on two or more lines, can provide even better access than ordinary stations to retail activities in their vicinity.

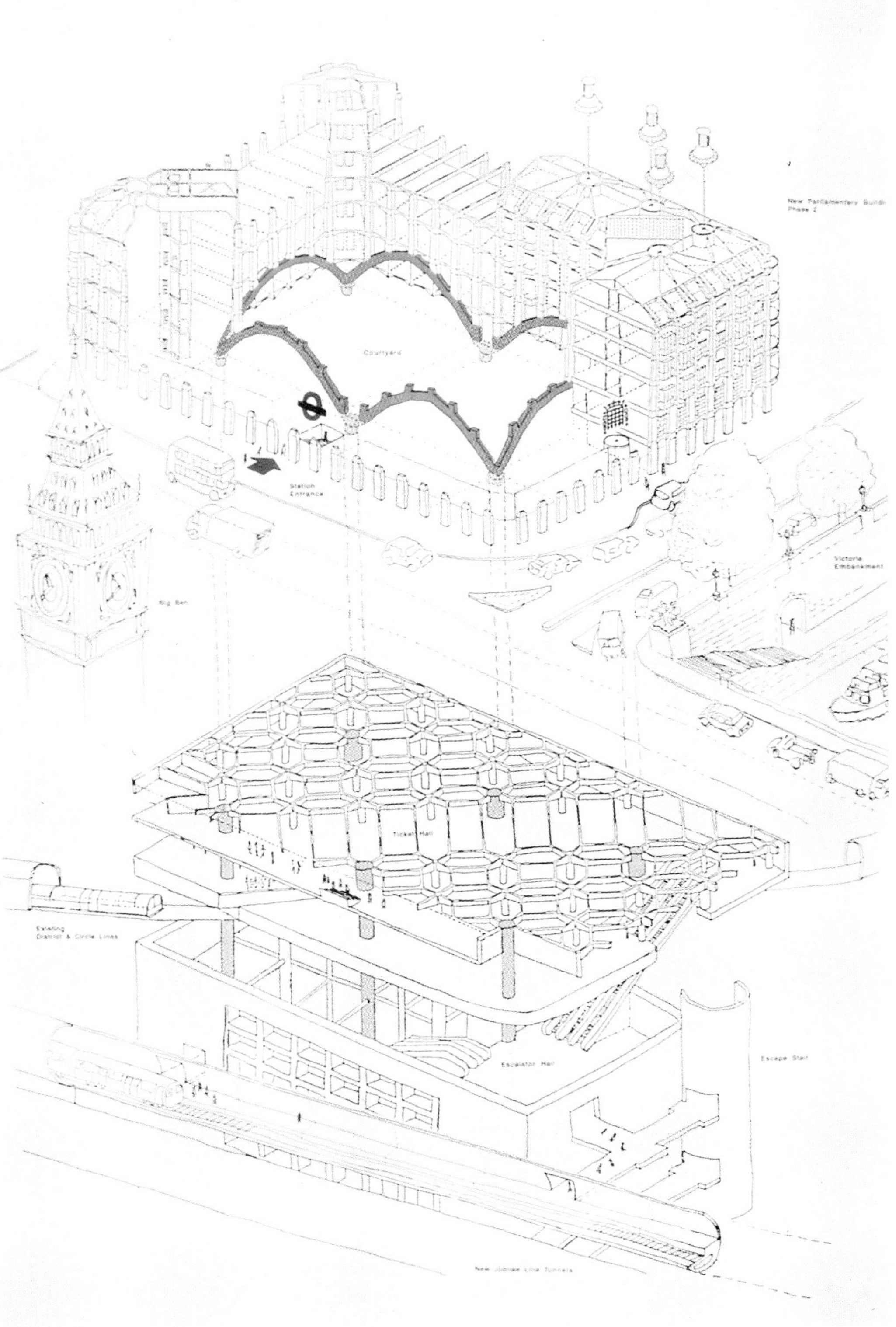

11. "Passimeter" and old manual ticket barrier at Hammersmith District Line ticket hall, 1956.

12. Ticket office with machines and Barclaybank machine at Baker Street built into the wall formerly occupied by W.H. Smith & Son and "Luncheon and Tearoom" and with old tiling preserved. Photo Ian Bell.

13. Travelcard zones map and/or bus fare zones map, 1995.

14. Old tickets with strictly defined route.

11

12

However, if the retail units are outside the ticket barrier (or outside LT Property), it may not be possible for all interchanging passengers to use various retail facilities; to an extent this depends on the type of ticket held and type of interchange. Of the three broad categories of interchange in London described below the *most* convenient for passengers provides the *least* access to retail facilities and the least amount of management information about travel patterns (and vice versa).

Cross-Platform/Same Level/Same Platform Interchange

At many locations served by the underground, passengers can transfer (a) between London Underground lines, (b) between London Underground and British Rail services, or (c) between London Underground and Docklands Light Railway services by walking across an "island" platform onto another train (normally headed in the same direction) or by boarding a following train on the same platform. Aldgate East and Ealing Common are examples of same-platform interchange.

"Cross platform" interchange, where the alignment of the tracks and platforms concerned allows it to be provided, has many benefits: the amount of time between leaving one train and boarding the next can be very little indeed. Cross/same platform interchange is likely to be most convenient for those with mobility impairments, a better distribution of passengers along each train can be achieved (i.e. not clustered around platform entrance/exit locations) and, because of the strong visual links, the need for explanatory signs is minimised.

Most of these benefits apply also to "same level interchange" where the two platforms are in parallel tunnels and passengers interchange via a series of cross-passages. The same-level interchange between the Victoria Line and the City Branch of the Northern Line at Euston is unusual in that passengers alight from one train and continue their journeys on another train leaving the adjacent platform in the opposite direction.

The more convenient interchange that the Victoria Line has with the City Branch (compared with the Charing Cross Branch) helped redress the previous imbalance of demand between the two Northern Line branches and enabled the Northern Line to be scheduled more efficiently.

Cross-platform or same-level interchange offers the least scope for retail development: space limitations underground or on an island platform mean that there is rarely room for more than a small kiosk, telephones, chocolate machines.

"Behind the Barrier" Interchange

Where the vertical and/or horizontal alignment of tracks and platforms at a given station does not allow cross platform/same level interchange, a pedestrian route may be provided via passageways, stairs, escalators and lifts without requiring the passenger to pass through a ticket barrier. Many of these interchanges are achieved at low level.

In some cases, separate Underground stations were originally built by different companies and a "behind the barrier" connection was created later in order to make interchange and/or automatic fare collection easier.

Examples of formerly separate stations now merged as interchanges are Notting Hill Gate, South Kensington, Charing Cross (formerly "Trafalgar Square" and "Strand") and Gloucester Road. Bank and Monument stations are physically merged but, unusually, retain different names.

When Central Line platforms were built at Holborn to provide "behind the barrier" interchange with the Piccadilly Line, British Museum station was closed.

"Out of Station" Interchange

There are a few Underground stations in London where interchange passengers between some lines are still required to exit through one ticket barrier and re-enter through another, this interchange route being a public area and/or used by other pedestrians. Remaining examples are Paddington (interchange between the Hammersmith & City Line and District/Circle/Bakerloo Lines), King's Cross St Pancras (interchange between Metropolitan/Hammersmith & City/Circle Lines and Northern/Victoria/Piccadilly Lines) and Hammersmith (interchange between Hammersmith & City and District/Piccadilly Lines), which is one of the case studies investigated at the end of this article.

Many of the interchanges between Main Line termini and London Underground are also of the "out of station" type. This type of interchange is the *least* convenient for passengers but it provides the most exposure to any retail units en route.

Being outside the ticket barrier, the retail units are accessible to non-travellers as well as to interchanging passengers.

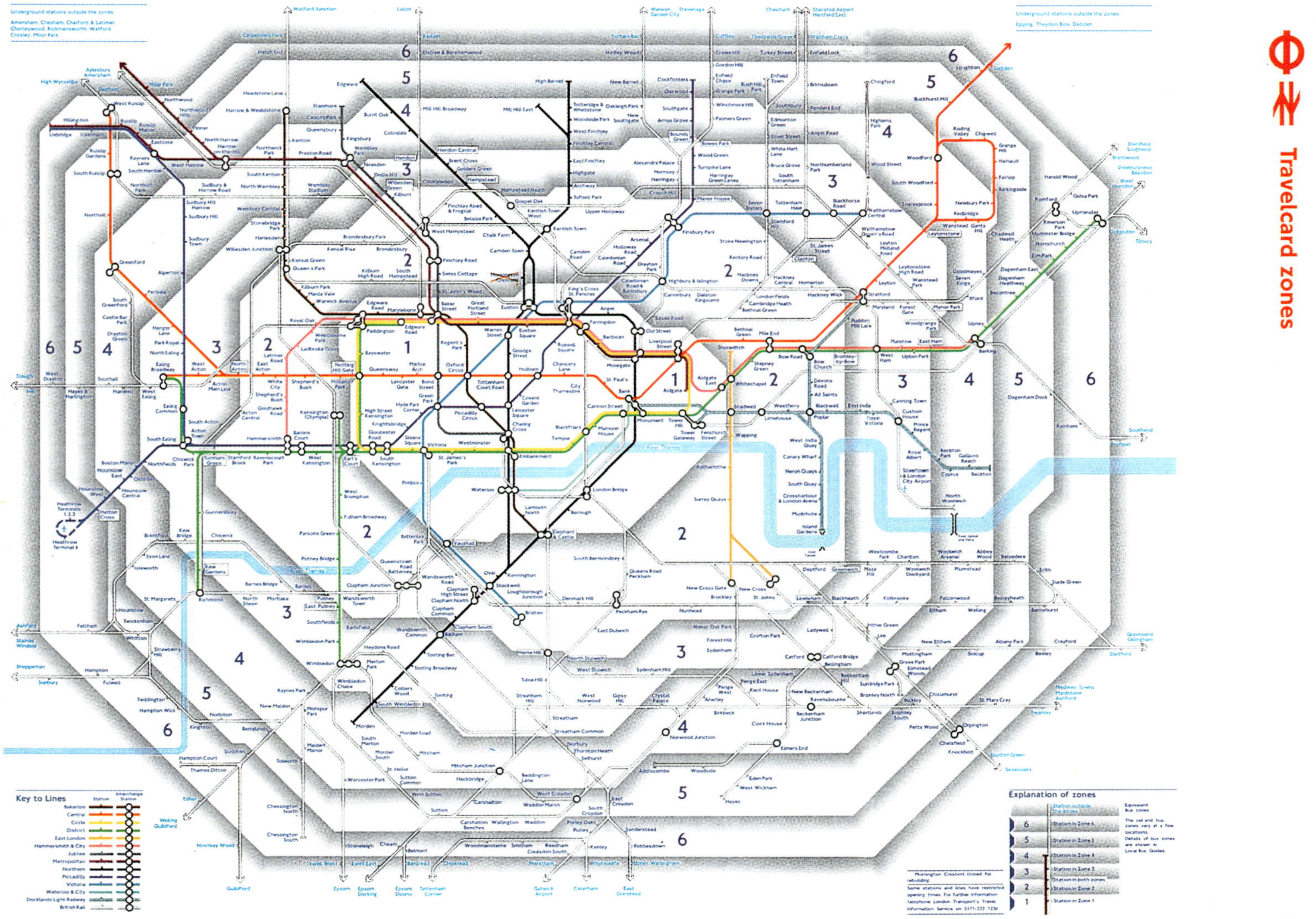
Travelcard zones
Key to Lines
Explanation of zones

13

WOOD GREEN
6d to
Highgate
(change Finsbury Park)
Farringdon
Euston
(change Kings Cross)
Cockfosters
Old Street
or intermediately
MAR
3rd Cl. L.P.T. BOARD
BANK
2nd CLASS MONTHLY SEASON TICKET BETWEEN
EDGWARE
and BOND STREET
via Goodge Street & change Tottenham Ct. Rd.
19 JUN 71
Holder's Name
Edgware
FOR CONDITIONS SEE BACK
233
7 13586
LONDON PASSENGER TRANSPORT BOARD
LONDON BRIDGE
2d
3rd Cl.

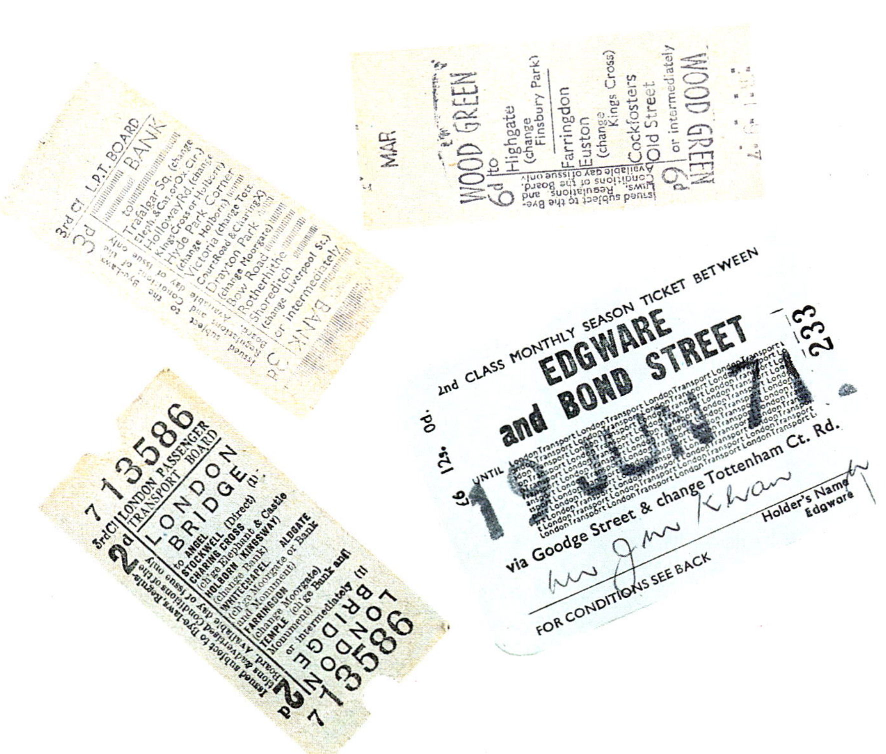

14

Euston

A terminus for the London & Birmingham Railway was opened on this site in 1837. Separate underground station entrances were opened here in 1907. One was built for the City & South London Railway in what is now Eversholt Street. The other, for the Hampstead Tube, was in Melton Street. Low-level connections were provided between the underground stations and the main line station. The 1907 station entrances were closed in 1914. The separate underground lines were eventually merged to form what is now called the Northern Line.

The modernisation and overhead electrification of the main line station and construction of the Victoria Line in the 1960s caused both stations to be rebuilt and a new bus station to be constructed at street level.

The access arrangements direct from the main line stations and suburban platforms to the Underground have many advantages but it is now impractical/uneconomic to provide access to the Underground station when the main line station is closed (on public holidays around Christmas for example) but the Underground is open. A compromise solution is to open the Underground station at such times for interchange between Underground Lines only. 20.5 million passengers entered or left the Underground system at Euston in 1995; nearly 10 million additional passengers used this station for interchange between Underground lines.

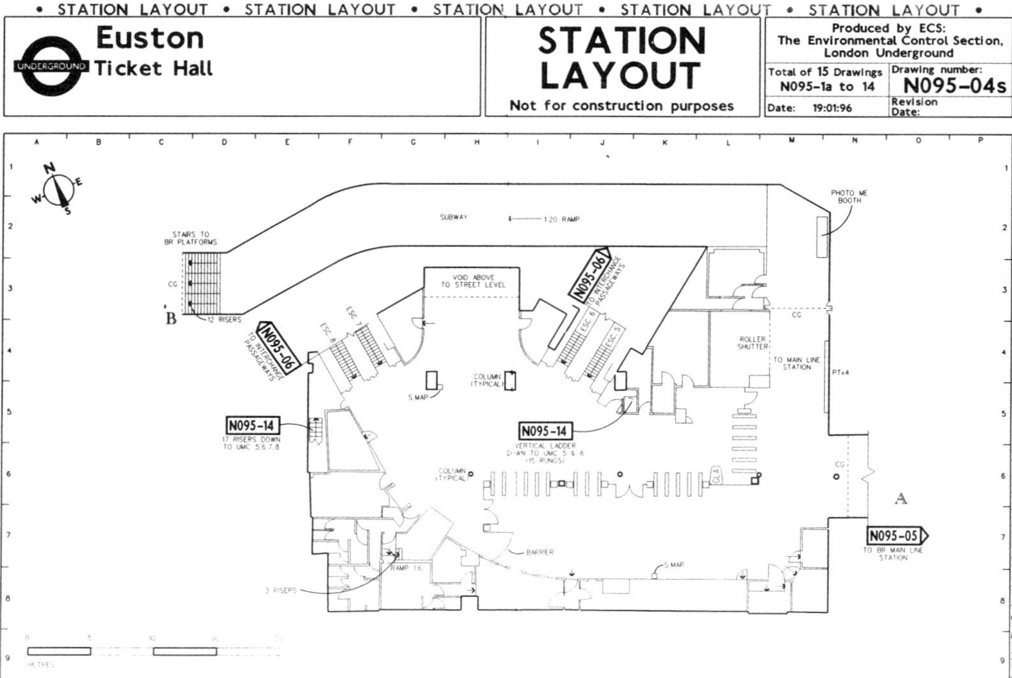

15. Ticket hall plan.

16. Entrance on the main line concourse which shows retailing on railtrack property.
Photo Ian Bell.

17. Axonometric.

Hammersmith

What is now the Hammersmith & City Line station opened in 1864. The District Railway station at Hammersmith Broadway opened in 1874; the Great Northern, Piccadilly & Brompton Railway (which became today's Piccadilly Line) arrived at Hammersmith Broadway in 1906.

Interchange between District and Piccadilly lines is cross-platform but between District/Piccadilly and Hammersmith & City lines involves passengers have to exit through the ticket barrier at one station and re-entering at the other: an "out of station" interchange.

For many years, the only reasonable way of crossing the busy road which separates the stations was via a public pedestrian subway. A step-free route is now also available over pedestrian crossings controlled by traffic lights.

There were experimental automatic exit gates at the old District & Piccadilly Lines station, especially chosen to challenge the "out of station" ticketing problems.

There were unsuccessful proposals to redevelop the Hammersmith Broadway site, to improve interchange between the separate stations, and incorporate a new bus station.

The scheme actually built is substantially different. There are now lifts and escalators between bus station level and ticket hall level. There are separate lifts between ticket hall level and District & Piccadilly platform level.

19. Ticket barrier, 1967.

18. Exterior view, 1933.

20. Ticket barrier, 1996.
Photo Ian Bell.

21. Exterior view with buses approaching.

Baker Street

Opened in 1863 on the world's first underground section, this is almost the only station on that first section to have retained its original name as well as its world-famous associations with the – fictional – Sherlock Holmes who is represented on some of the tiling. The station is now served by five London Underground lines with a total of 10 platforms all below the surface, more Underground platforms than at any other station. In 1995, 22 million passengers used this station to interchange between Underground lines; additionally 21 million entered or left the Underground system here.

The station has many retail units both inside and outside the ticket barrier. Two units were converted into a ticket office in 1987 but their fascias were restored. The 1863 platforms (now numbered 5 and 6) have also been restored.

"Same level" interchange is now provided: (i) between the northbound Bakerloo and northbound Jubilee Lines; (ii) between the southbound Bakerloo and southbound Jubilee Lines; (iii) between the eastbound Hammersmith & City/Circle platform and Metropolitan Line platforms 1 and 2. Other interchange between Underground lines at this station is of the "behind the barrier" type.

A former Luggage Lift between street, concourse and subsurface platform level is now used to supply the retail units and for mobility-impaired passenger use.

22. Metropolitan Railway, today.

23. Platform with Sherlock Holmes profile on the wall.
Photo Ian Bell.

24. Metropolitan Railway, 1863.

Bond Street

The original Central London Railway station (on the south side of Oxford Street) opened with the line in 1900. Selfridges department store (on the north side) opened in 1909: there have been proposals to rename the station "Selfridges". A legend concerns a direct pedestrian subway connection between the store and the station!

Originally there was a ground-level entrance to the modest ticket hall from which there were two escalators, one up from and one down towards platform level. The Central Line runs east-west at this point, beneath and following Oxford Street, which is now one of the busiest retail areas in the world.

The station was rebuilt with the initial construction of the Jubilee Line (which opened in 1979 and follows a north-south orientation at this location – ruling out "same-level" interchange) and in anticipation of the West One Shopping Development. The larger ticket hall is now incorporated into the basement level of the development and access is available from the North Side of Oxford Street as well as from the retail area. There are now 8 escalators within the Underground station (i.e. not counting those in the retail area). One objective of the new Bond Street station was to relieve access, egress and interchange pressure on Oxford Circus station nearby. 22 million passengers entered or left the Underground system at Bond Street in 1995; nearly 8 million additional passengers used this station for interchange between lines.

Bond Street station will gain more importance when the Jubilee Line Extension is inaugurated and could gain even more as a proposed CrossRail interchange.

25. Exterior view, 1952.

26. Present-day view from Oxford Street.
Photo Ian Bell.

27. The basement level containing the West One Shopping Development and the ticket machines.
Photo Ian Bell.

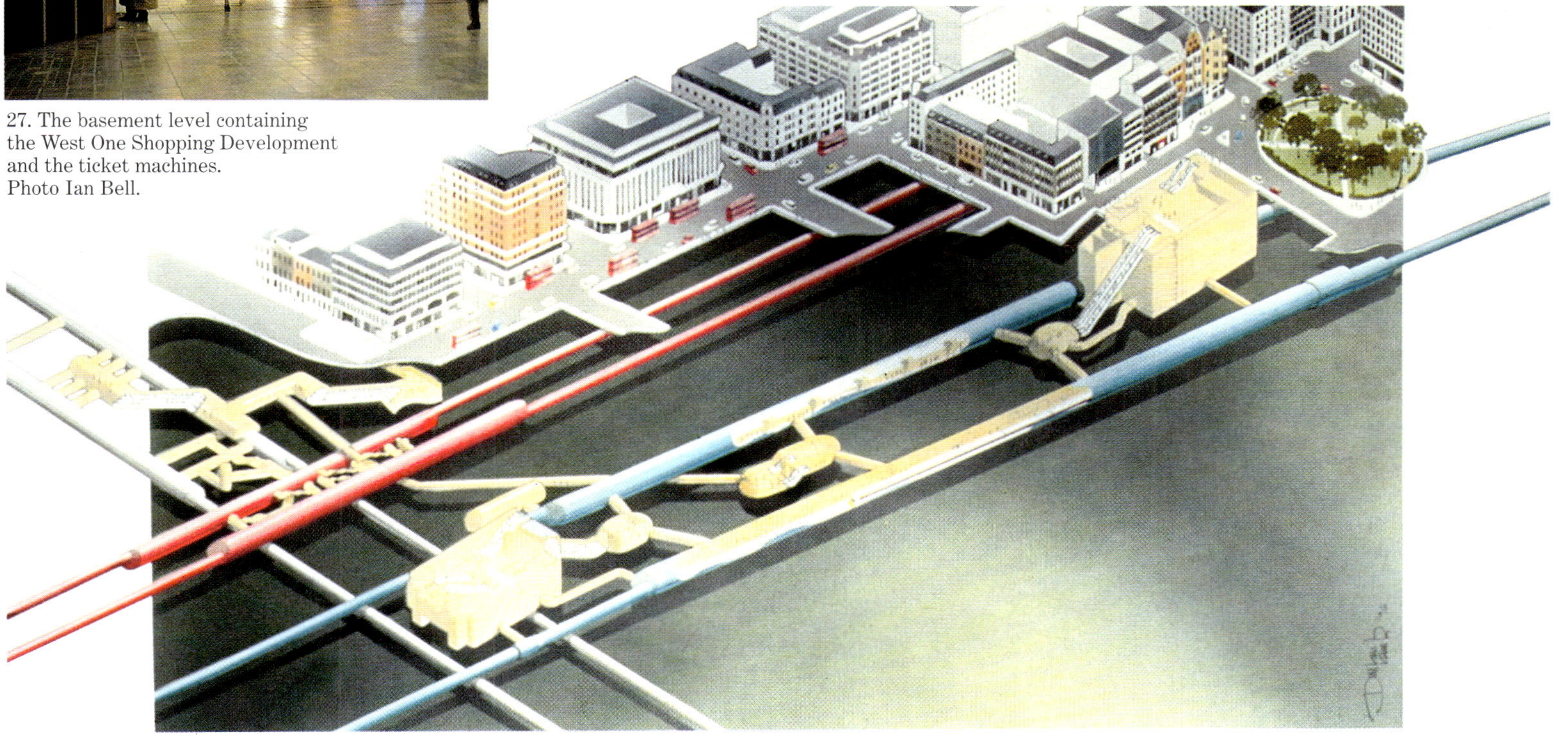

28. Axonometric of the proposed CrossRail interchange.

Liverpool Street

Broad Street "main line" station was built adjacent to this site in 1865. That at Liverpool Street opened here in 1874 and a connection with the Metropolitan Line was made one year later: trains from Hammersmith ran right into the Great Eastern platforms as did trains from the East London Line at times. Both these connections have been severed. At tube level, the Central London Railway terminated here between 1912 and 1946. Broad Street station was closed in 1984 to make way for the Broadgate development (by Rosehaugh Stanhope in conjunction with the British Rail Property Board) which involved rebuilding both Liverpool Street stations (main line and Underground).

The many cramped Underground ticket halls and offices were replaced with fewer, larger ticket halls and offices. A lift is now provided between street, Railtrack concourse and Underground concourse levels. Passengers interchanging between main line and Underground can now benefit from the very substantial retailing on the Railtrack concourse and in the Shopping Arcade. Liverpool Street is a considerable destination in its own right being located in the heart of the City of London with great areas of office space within walking distance: 60 trains currently arrive in the main line station's 18 platforms during the peak hour. Express trains to/from Stansted Airport now terminate here. There is substantial interchange between the main lines and the four Underground Lines which currently serve this station. A new bus station is also incorporated. 42 million passengers used the Underground station in 1995; fewer than 4 million interchanged between Underground lines here.

29. One of the many entrances, 1939.

30. One of the many entrances, 1939.

31. Old manual ticket barrier, 1939.

32. New ticket hall, with machines built into the wall, barriers and retailing. Photo Ian Bell.

Heathrow Terminals 1, 2, 3

(originally called "Heathrow Central")

Heathrow has been the busiest airport in the world in terms of international passengers for many years and, in 1977, became the first international airport to have its own underground link. The station was built between the three terminal buildings then existing and connected to each by a network of subways radiating from the station concourse. The station was thus equally accessible to passengers of all airlines.

The station complex was constructed on four levels with its platforms at the lowest. The next level up contains staff accommodation and plant rooms and is not accessible to the public. Above that is the concourse level reached by escalators to and from the platforms. Above concourse level is a Bus and Coach station. There is a passenger-operated lift between Bus/Coach station and concourse level. There is another lift between platform and concourse level.

The new name of "Heathrow Terminals 1, 2, 3" was phased in when Terminal 4 and its separate Underground station opened.

11.35 million passengers used this station in 1995; another 2 million entered/left the Underground system at Terminal 4. Journey times to/from Central London are admittedly slow compared with the 16 minutes proposed between Heathrow Central Area and Paddington for the Heathrow Express, now under construction. For many passengers, this is and will continue to be offset by the higher frequency of the Underground (up to 12 trains per hour at Heathrow) and the large number of stations through the centre of London which the Piccadilly Line serves directly. With 18 years' experience, there are plans now to modernise this Piccadilly Line/airport interchange with staff receiving special customer care training, the selling of Underground tickets in the baggage reclaim area of Terminal 1, new signs, improved sight lines and a "fast track" for regular customers who know the interchange. There will also be a substantial revision for retail sales arrangements at this station. Piccadilly Line train speeds will be improved marginally and the 12 trains per hour peak frequency will be scheduled 7 days a week. It is proposed to extend the Piccadilly Line to Terminal 5 if the latter is built.

33. Artist's impression of the airport-Underground station interchange.

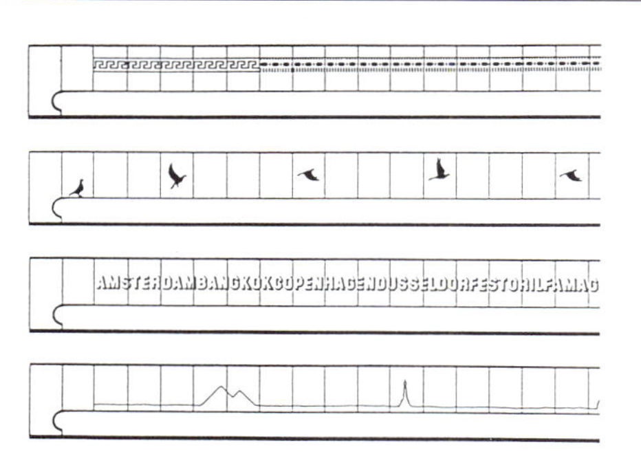

34. Murals along the moving walkways connecting the Underground station to the three terminal buildings.

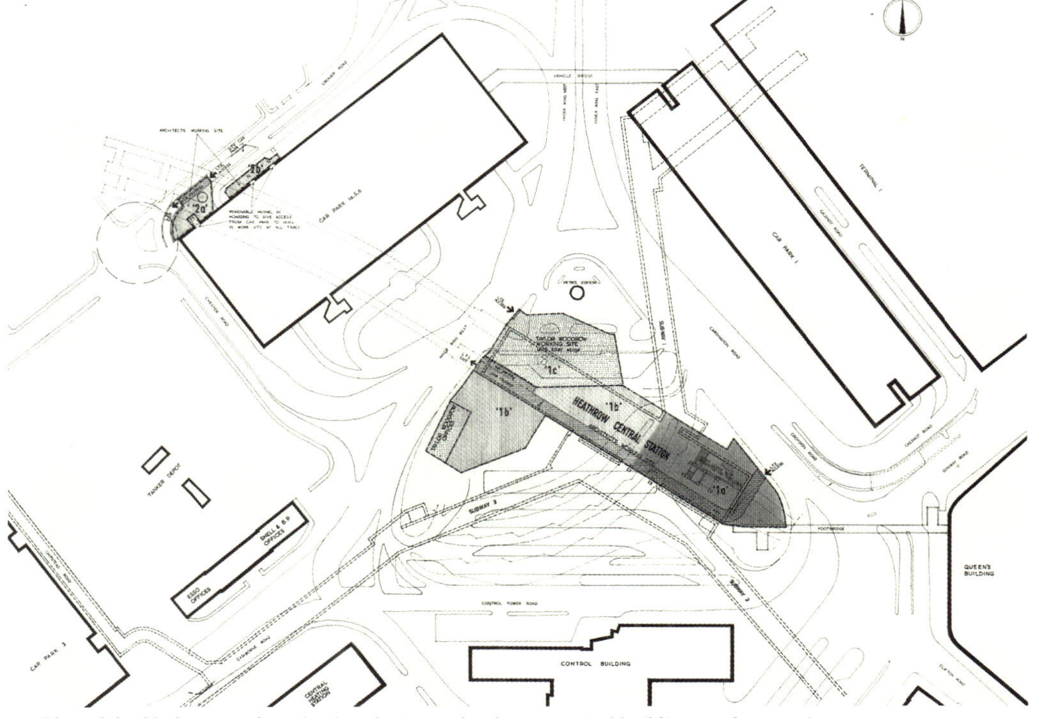

35. Plan of the Underground station in relation to the three terminal buildings and car parks.

Gordon Hafter

London's Underground. How The Physical and Environmental Origins Have Affected Its Technology and Operations

Glossary of Terms

London Transport: The general name (apart from legal purposes) by which the London Passenger Transport Board, later The London Transport Executive, later the London Transport board, and currently London Regional Transport are all known

London Underground: The present Company operating the Underground, (legally London Underground Limited) a wholly owned subsidiary of London Regional Transport, which is the umbrella body for both London Underground and London Buses.

London's Underground: A loose term meaning all those railways currently forming "London Underground", together with those which at the time being described were under the legal ownership of other bodies such as the London and North Eastern Railway, The Great Western Railway and other joint organisations such as the Metropolitan and Great Central Joint Committee and the East London Rail-

way Joint Committee. It includes for this purpose parts of the underground system still owned and often partly operated by British Railways, such as that part of the District Line between Gunnersbury and Richmond.

underground: (with a lower case initial "u"). A less formal version of London's Underground.

Underground: (with an upper case initial "U"). Means those lines actually owned at the time being described by London Transport (q.v.) or its predecessors.

The Circle Line: that line formed by parts of the former Metropolitan Railway and pert of the former Metropolitan District Railway which together form a circle round inner London. This was formerly known as the "Inner Circle" to differentiate it from the "Middle" and "Outer" circles which were not complete circles at all and were formed partly of underground lines and partly of other railways' lines.

The Central Line: that line formed from the Central London Railway, and the Ealing and Shepherd's Bush Railway plus extensions over parts of other railways.

The District Line: the former Metropolitan District Railway plus certain sections taken over from the London and South Western and the London, Tilbury and Southend Railways together with those parts of British Railways run over by District Line trains.

The names and origins of other lines are largely self explanatory.

Metropolitan railways have taken many forms throughout the world, though as the pace of construction increased during the third quarter of the 20th century, many of the more recent constructions have embodied common practices resulting from the refinement of experience. Nevertheless, projects continue to exhibit individual characteristics born out of

1

1. A Liner express train and a Metropolitan Line electrically hauled train running side by side on one of the four tracked sections before all four tracks were electrified.

2. Poster for "Met Steam 1994".

urban environments, political situations and cultures which have nurtured them, as well as those arising from national attitudes and the level of economic development of the countries in which they are located.

Perhaps nowhere is this more striking than in London. Not only was it the first metropolitan railway to be built, and therefore had to be constructed without any guiding precedents, but its initial environment was unique at the time and it has remained distinctive since.

Although guided waggonways (with animal traction and primarily for mineral transport) had appeared in various European countries by the end of the 18th century, the "railway", properly so-called, providing a "common carrier" function for any passengers or goods offering themselves for carriage originated in England.

Here the industrial revolution was already well underway a quarter of a century before it became well established elsewhere, with a resulting explosion in urban population. Thus a countrywide railway system had largely been constructed by the 1850s, when many other European countries were still served only by a number of unconnected lines.

Great Britain was then also the richest and most powerful nation state, having an empire larger than any other power. The resulting commerce was a prime cause of London becoming the world's largest city, and the first to experience the frustrations of traffic congestion. But as will be seen later, this feature, a prime mover in the construction of other metros (and the expansion of London's later on), had almost no influence on the original project. It must be remembered that "London" was (and is) not one city, but a collection of "villages" plus two cities – the City of London, and the City of Westminster, some 3 km apart. When we now talk of the City (with a capital C), we mean the City of London.

A further, quite early feature of London's expansion was low rise and, (for the epoch), low density suburban building, with many streets of small houses which differed from the five and six storey apartment blocks being built in similarly expanding cities such as Glasgow, Paris and Vienna.

The British economy was also, like that of the United States and unlike much of the rest of Europe, among the least regulated of those in the then developed world, and all its railways, like other industrial enterprises, had been established by private enterprise with little state planning.

Join us for a day in May and relive the sight, the sound and the thrill of steam with the Metropolitan Line's special steam-hauled trains.

Saturday 21 and Sunday 22 May - every 45 minutes Watford to Amersham (calling at Rickmansworth, where you can ride the free bus service to the nearby canal event).

Saturday 28, Sunday 29 and Monday 30 May - every hour Harrow-on-the-Hill to Amersham non-stop. (There will also be one special train from Wembley Park to Uxbridge on 28, 29 and 30 May leaving Wembley Park at 09.10 and Uxbridge at 09.57.)

Unlimited daily steam tickets available for travel on any train cost £6 Adult, and £3 Child (£8 for the Uxbridge trips). You can buy tickets in advance by post or on the day at Amersham, Watford and Harrow-on-the-Hill stations.
For further details write to "Steam on the Met" at London Underground, 13 Allsop Place, London NW1 5LJ, or telephone 071-918 9436 for a pre-recorded message.

3. The original Metropolitan Railway
in 1863. Note the three rails
to accommodate standard and broad
gauge trains.

56

3

4

57

But some common standards had early been adopted for business reasons, including a common gauge (apart from the Great Western Railway), as well as common coupling and buffing arrangements, which enabled through running from one system to another.

Also, uniquely in Europe, most of the principal railways had, from the start, adopted a common high platform level, enabling rapid and easy boarding and alighting to be effected. To this day, only Ireland and the Netherlands have universal high platforms as in Britain, whereas elsewhere these are often confined to principal stations, (if provided at all) and to urban systems.

It was the demands of commerce, not congestion which brought pressure to provide a much speedier means than cabs and horse omnibuses for businessmen to reach the City, and a railway from Paddington, Euston and King's Cross Stations seemed the obvious solution, given that all these main line termini were between 3 and 7 km from the City itself.

There did not seem to be any overwhelming reason why this railway should be different in its physical standards, its signalling or its rolling stock from those already adopted for short distance traffic in Great Britain generally.

In fact a shortage of capital required it to hire its coaches and locomotives from one of the existing railways, at least until it was firmly established, and therefore to be connected to at least one of them. In fact it was connected to two of them, both of which saw it primarily as a means of getting their own passengers to the City.

Thus it was that the first underground railway in London was projected in 1845, partly with the objects already described, but with support from the City Corporation who were anxious to provide a cogent reason for demolishing a part of the slum area around the Fleet river valley.

It was 10 years before the various proposals took the final shape of a railway from Bishop's Road at Paddington to Farringdon on the western edge of the City of London, (some 6 km) and joined at the outset to both the Great Western Railway, the only broad gauge – 7 ft – (actually 2140 mm) line in Britain and the standard gauge (1435 mm) Great Northern Railway. It was a further 8 years before it was completed, and was therefore built to mixed gauge (with 3 rails) and of course, steam traction was the only means available.

London, unlike Paris, grew early at the suburban fringe, with little affordable accommodation in the central built up area. Thus the

5

6

7. The City and South London Railway, the very first "tube" line as it was in the 1890s.

8. A "tube" car in the 1930s. Until 1938, it was not possible to fit traction equipment and motors between the low floor and rails, so the underframe had to be "cranked" over the motor bogie, and the equipment housed in a special compartment above it.

58

underground soon saw its function and opportunities as extending or linking itself up with suburban branches of the main line railways, to bring workers to the centre.

This continues to differentiate it from the Métro (urbain) of Paris, or New York's Subway, which still serve heavily populated inner city areas. Thus longer average interstation distances to keep up the commercial speeds needed for the longer average journeys in London also affected both design and operational constraints.

Steam required the system to be built near the surface for ventilation purposes, with as many open sections as possible and as London streets in general were rather narrow, extension of the system was limited, difficult and caused great and much resented disruption. It took over 30 years for even the present limited sub-surface system to be completed.

Elevated railways, as in New York and later Hamburg, (the Hamburg underground is still known officially as the Hamburger Hochbahn, or Hamburg Elevated Railway) though cheaper but environmentally unfriendly, were impractical over London's streets, thus much of the real centre remained unserved until the end of the 19th century when the advent of electric traction enabled deep level railways to be considered.

Fortuitously, central London rests very largely on a bed of impervious but soft clay. This layer is ideal for bored tunnels constructed by shield methods some 12 to 30 metres below the surface, so it was possible to provide further underground lines once electric traction had eliminated the need for smoke and steam dispersal.

Thus the "tubes" or smaller diameter tunnels with specialised rolling stock came into existence as a "second wave" system. Most of them were promoted by separate companies which nearly all got quickly into financial difficulties.

Three of them, the Great Northern Piccadilly and Brompton Railway (itself formed out of two even smaller projects – the Great Northern and Strand Railway and the Brompton and Piccadilly Circus Railway), the Baker Street and Waterloo Railway and the Charing Cross, Euston and Hampstead Railway, were soon combined into a new company called the London Electric Railway, owned by Underground Electric Railways of London Ltd., a company formed to buy up and electrify the Metropolitan District Railway.

These companies became known as the Underground Group of Companies.

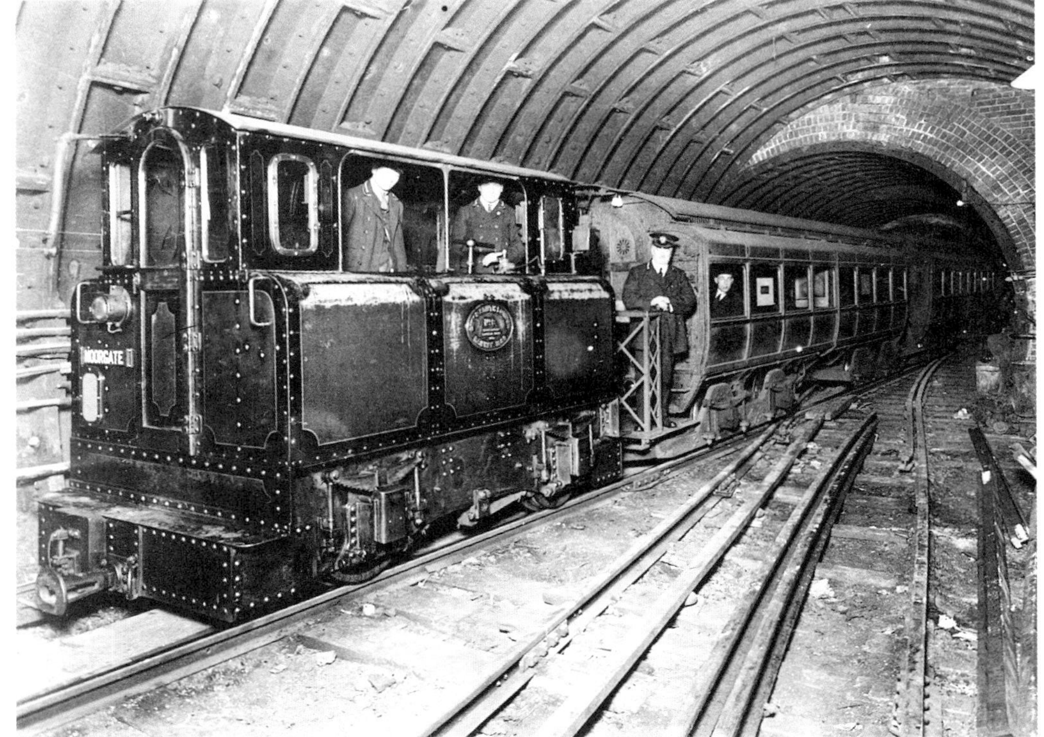

7

8

Much later on, the Underground Group absorbed also the Central London Railway (the nucleus of the present Central Line which operated a flat fare system in its independent days so that it became known as "The Twopenny Tube"), and the City and South London Railway, which also started with a flat fare and is now the City Branch and Morden section of the Northern Line.

South of the river, this stratum of clay is much less general, which is one (though not the only) reason why the Underground has developed to a more limited extent on that side of the Thames. Only now, in the 1990s is an East-West "tube" line being built south of the river Thames, as the Jubilee Line Extension project.

No government or city finance was provided. There was, and is, no overall municipal authority covering the whole built-up London area, apart from the brief period of the Greater London Council (1963-1986), although there was a much smaller area covered by a single authority, called the London County Council which existed from 1888 until 1963. However this covered only the area of central London and a small part of the surrounding built up area, and not Greater London. So until the late 1920s and the formation of the London Passenger Transport Board in 1933, lines were only built where commercial considerations dictated. The Metropolitan Railway in any case remained outside the Underground Group until that time.

Profitability required linking these new tube lines with existing railways' suburban branches, building their own suburban extensions, or linking with the older (formerly steam operated) sub-surface underground lines. This made the London underground, particularly in its operational methods, always much more "railway" like, than the metros of other large cities, some of which developed from tramway organisations.

Today the Réseau Express Régional (RER) in Paris displays some of that philosophy of London's underground, but in a modern and developed way, while the Underground has been adopting some of the "exclusive" features of other metros.

As late as 1960, the underground was still operating a number of locomotive hauled trains, hauled by electric locomotives as far as Rickmansworth and thence by steam locomotives owned by British Railways out to Aylesbury, some 70 km from their starting point at Liverpool Street on the Circle Line in the City of London. These trains had guards

9

10

60 and baggage compartments, where heavy luggage could be conveyed as well as parcels and newspaper traffic, indistinguishable from main-line practice.

So did some of the electric multiple-unit trains, and to this day, certain lines operate fast and semi-fast trains which do not call at all stations, a practice otherwise found on a considerable scale only in New York, but there invariably aided by the availability of four tracks on the sections concerned.

For the same reasons, the fares system on the underground has always been generally similar to that of the rest of Britain's railways, and through bookings to stations often well outside the suburban area using routes of both London Underground and British Railways are common.

Through tickets generally between towns involving journeys across London, (even international tickets to cities such as Birmingham) automatically include in their validity the journey on the Underground between mainline termini in London. They may also be used via the many other interchange stations between the underground and British Railways.

Similarly, many underground lines in the suburbs carried goods traffic, and had goods stations alongside the passenger stations. Some of these were operated by the underground itself, for example all that part of the underground which was still the Metropolitan Railway operated goods trains to most of its stations in the suburban area, using its own steam locomotives, even after electrification of the passenger services. After the formation of the London Passenger Transport Board, this work was handed over to a main line railway, but the services remained.

At the same time, other parts of the underground often provided facilities for goods traffic, including some goods stations right in the heart of London, the trains to which were operated by some of the main-line railway companies, and after nationalisation, by British Railways.

Anyone standing on a Circle Line platform between Edgware road and Farringdon about 21.00 hours would, as late as the 1960s, have seen goods trains carrying the capital's meat, hauled by BR locos, travelling over the Circle Line between passenger trains on their way to Smithfield market, the City's central meat market which had its own goods station below ground situated between Farringdon and Barbican stations.

Similarly, in the afternoons, there were goods trains to large depots at West Ken-

11

12

13

14. A map issued by the Metropolitan
Railway before it was absorbed into
the London Passenger Transport Board,
showing all the underground lines
in operation at the end of the 1920s.

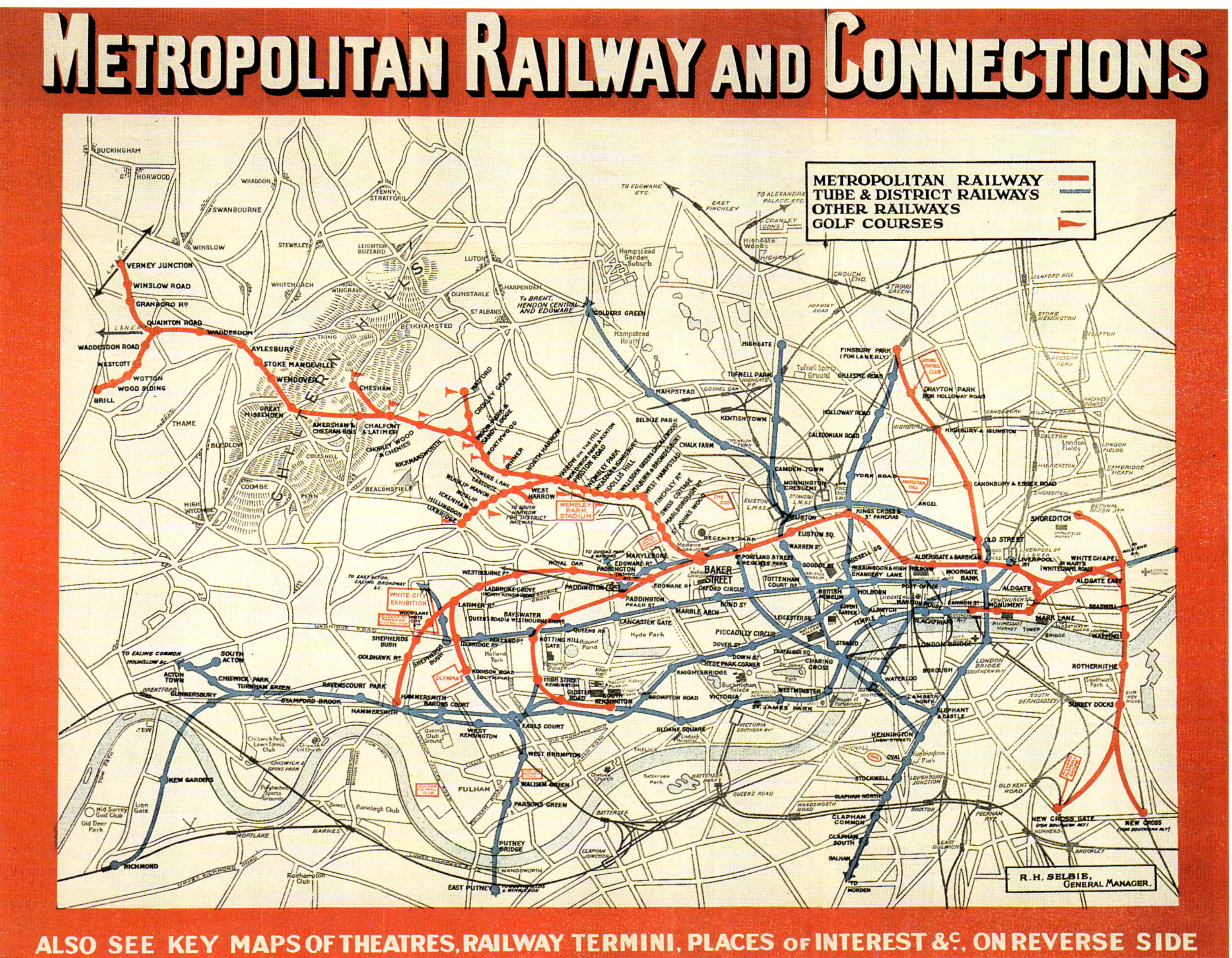

62 sington and High Street Kensington on the
District Line.

During the 1930s, the government, in an effort to combat unemployment, financed the "1935-40 New Works Programme", which included some new suburban extensions of the Underground, and also some further connections between the Underground and main-line railways in East, North and West London, with the passenger services being taken over by Underground trains.

On these lines, operational control of which also passed to the Underground, the goods services were left in the hands of the former owners of the railways concerned, and so the connections with the rest of those systems remained.

As a result, those connections were used not only for the goods traffic, but also at week-ends in the summer time for excursion trains to the coast.

Thus it was not unusual to see on summer Sunday mornings, steam or diesel hauled excursion trains formed of main-line railway coaches to places like Clacton or Southend-on-Sea calling at stations on the Northern Line between High Barnet and East Finchley, or on the Central Line between Epping and Leyton, in between tube trains.

Until the outbreak of the Second World War in 1939, the District Line too used to operate at least one through train from Ealing Broadway to Southend-on-Sea (over 70 km) all the year round every day. The coaches used belonged to the London Midland and Scottish (LMS) Railway, and were hauled by District Line electric locomotives as far as Barking, where LMS steam locos took over.

Every weekday, until the Second World War, there were through trains to the City in the peak hours from Slough, and Windsor, over 40 km from the City, formed of Great Western coaches and hauled by Great Western steam locos as far as Paddington, and thence by Metropolitan Line electric locos over the Circle Line.

Steam and later diesel trains of British Railways continued even after the Second World War to operate over that part of the Circle Line known as "Widened Lines" between King's Cross and Moorgate which was 4 tracked, although two of the tracks have now been handed over to British Railways, and electrified by them on the 25 KV overhead system. This is the reverse of the situation referred to above, when, during the 1930s certain sections of the main line railways suburban systems were handed over to the Underground.

15

The Metropolitan Railway, although the original underground railway, in fact always regarded itself as a "real" main line railway, eventually stretching far out into the countryside to reach Verney Junction and Brill, both nearly 90 km from central London.

Part of this line was built primarily to make a junction with the "London Extension" of the Great Central Railway, at Quainton Road, and carried Great Central express trains over its tracks almost all the way to London.

The Great Central's chairman was Edward Watkin, who also chaired the Metropolitan and the South Eastern Railway, which owned the line from London via Ashford to Folkestone and Dover, and was a promoter of the Channel Tunnel project.

He saw the Great Central as part of a grand line from Manchester to Paris, and so being built late, opportunity was taken to build the Great Central (and the Metropolitan extension to meet it apart from the low Finchley Road tunnels), to the slightly larger clearances then common in France, before the Berne convention on loading gauge set the "Universal" loading gauge for international rolling stock in Europe, the precursor of the present

International Union of Railways (UIC) "A" loading gauge.

As mentioned at the beginning of this article, the original line from Bishops Road to Farringdon was also built to wide clearances as the Great Western Railway which supplied the original rolling stock was broad gauge, (2140 mm) with wide rolling stock to suit.

Thus the whole Metropolitan Line of the London Underground is still able to operate the widest, though not the highest rolling stock in Britain.

Its "real railway" image was further fostered by the Metropolitan Railway, and its successor the Metropolitan Line of the Underground by providing, until the outbreak of war in 1939, some peak hour trains each way between the City and both Chesham and Aylesbury which contained a 1st Class Pullman Car in which City directors could take their breakfasts on the way in, and drinks on the way home.

Those were the days when such gentlemen got to their offices at 10.00 and left again at 16.00. For a time the cars also operated in late evening trains designed to capture some of the theatre traffic returning to high class outer suburban areas served and developed by the Metropolitan Railway between Harrow and Aylesbury. This area was marketed as "Metroland".

Thus although the very restricted clearances of the "tube" lines produced rolling stock which was of special construction, the connections with main line railways dictated the signalling and operating practices which were very similar.

Indeed most employees of the Underground are considered to be "railwaymen" and enjoy similar (if not identical) travel facilities to main line railwaymen within the United Kingdom and Ireland, even if not in the rest of Europe, unlike staff of other metros.

Thus there are many parts of London's Underground which started life or continue to be part of the mainline railway system of the country, while some lines, originally part of the Underground now form part of, or are worked by British Railways.

The process of adjustment is still not complete, in that the new project for "CrossRail" a high capacity line linking East and West London with a high speed RER type new line through the centre will be worked by British Rail (or its privatised successors) at its two ends which are part of the existing BR network, but will have the stations and infrastructure of its central section in tunnel

16, 17. Exterior and interior
of Metropolitan Line first class
Pullman car.

across London, worked and maintained by London Underground.

It is a fair generalisation to say that it is only the central sections of the "tube" lines, (the Bakerloo, Central, Jubilee, Northern and Piccadilly), together with those extensions reached only through "tube" sections – for example the Edgware Branch of the Northern Line – which have never seen either steam hauled passenger or goods trains, either regularly or for special reasons. Even today, steam, diesel, or electric locomotive hauled "nostalgia" trips are worked over non-tube sections during most summers.

It is this identification of London's Underground with the rest of the nation's railways which has given it a rather special atmosphere as well as affecting the technical requirements of its civil engineering, signalling, rolling stock, ticketing and to some extent training and working practices.

There are two contrary movements currently affecting such arrangements. They are the requirements to make journeys into and within urban areas more convenient and "seamless", which has resulted in interworking on the London pattern elsewhere, such as the RER in Paris, and light rail on DB lines as in Karlsruhe and Saarbrücken in Germany, while on the other hand, ATO (automatic train operation) plus ATP (automatic train protection), together with differing systems of electrification are tending to divide rail operations into watertight compartments with no interrunning facilities.

Professionals working on current urban and suburban projects (for example airport connections such as the Heathrow Express and the somewhat analogous projects in other cities such as Stockholm), could do much worse than spend a little time reading up the lessons provided by 140 years of development of London's Underground.

16

17

64 Though often a potent facilitator of suburban growth, in London the railway was rarely the primary cause. Other factors had to be present, notably ready availability of land suitable for housing, social and economic forces favourable to house building and, of course a sufficient demand. London's Underground railways did however bring particular characteristics into this scenario and were associated with perceptions of their special value as a mode of transit; these we shall identify later.

Begun even before the railway age, the outward spread of London did not gain pace until the latter part of the 19th century. It came to a halt in the troubled years 1915-22, before resuming with unprecedented vigour. Activity reached its highest level in 1932-7, when a strong demand for middle class housing co-existed with economic conditions favourable to construction at low cost.

Almost everyone in London's large salaried class then had sufficient marginal income to afford the new suburban houses appearing in quantity around stations with convenient services to central London workplaces. Although the local authorities (principally the London County Council) had undertaken large housing programmes in the outer areas in the 1920s, their pace slowed after 1927 and it was the private sector which completed the great bulk of London's suburban expansion between 1923 and 1940, reaching a record output of almost 73,000 houses in 1934.

In these new districts, the commonest type of house was the two-storey "semi-detached" (sharing a party wall with its neighbour), with entrance hall, two reception rooms and a tiny kitchen on the ground floor, two main bedrooms and a small one upstairs and a small rectangular rear garden plot. Other features were parades of shops, with residential flats above, and frequently one or more cinemas. In contrast to pre-1914, churches followed only slowly, often not appearing until after 1945. These new suburbs quickly formed around railway stations, linked old villages to stations, spread around existing communities, or even appeared on green field sites. They prospered most if within walking distance of good railway facilities to central London. Having started house purchase, commuters had no marginal income remaining to buy a motor car and with most commuting then radial, there was heavy reliance on rail transport.

Following the end of World War Two, planning legislation placed a "Green Belt" around London, thus bringing to an end the long period of relentless outward growth. Since no Un-

2

1. C. Shepherd, poster inviting use of the newly-opened Edgware extension, in this case to explore the lanes and woods of the nearby countryside by travelling on the feeder bus services.

2. Commuters returning from their offices to their new homes leave Edgware terminus just after midday on Saturday, 3 July 1926. Some are being greeted by their wifes and children. This station, with its attractive three-sided forecourt in "Roman" style, was subsequently somewhat rebuilt.

3. Suburban publicity. A. Kermode, Underground Railways Company poster of 1924 that invites those dwelling in the small and monotonous 19th century terrace housing of inner London to move out to a bright new house in the country, using the newly opened extension to Edgware.

derground line extended beyond this Green Belt, no further "Underground Suburbs" were possible after 1945.

Early Underground Suburbs

London's first Underground railways, the Metropolitan (from 1863) and the Metropolitan District (from 1868), in their shallow subways, were initially entirely confined to the existing built-up area. Then, from the late 1870s, surface extensions were projected into the western and north western outskirts of the capital. Both companies began to work services to the Thames-side town of Richmond in 1877. Two years later, District trains reached Ealing and Hounslow was served from 1883-4. To the north west, the Metropolitan arrived at Willesden in 1879, at Harrow in 1880, and at the small country town of Rickmansworth in 1887. District trains served Putney from 1880 and in 1889 crossed the Thames to reach Wimbledon.

Since there was suitable building land available around many of the new stations and because Underground trains were not only frequent but provided a seamless journey directly to the commercial, administrative and financial heart of London, many better-paid office workers and London professional men were persuaded to move into the new villas. This was not confined to the districts mentioned; whilst the Underground services had the special additional advantages noted, an outward migration was under way in other directions all around London, where conditions for suburban growth of this type were favourable and train services of conventional railways were acceptably fast and frequent.

Stimulated by the arrival of the Underground in 1879 and by the existence of main line suburban services which also used the central area Underground, Ealing saw its population rise from around 5,000 in 1863 to over 30,000 by the mid 1890s. At Willesden, where ample building land came on to the market, the Metropolitan Railway company became a participant in suburban development from 1881, laying out streets and arranging for housebuilding near its station. Whilst residential expansion along the Putney and Wimbledon extensions in the 1880s and 1890s was pronounced, the new open air Underground services to Harrow, Pinner, Rickmansworth and Hounslow proved less successful initially, probably because journeys to central London were longer and more expensive at a time when there was ample choice of new housing nearer the centre.

3

4. Edgware, 1923. The Underground Railway terminus is under construction in the centre, as is the first section of George Cross's Premier Parade shopping development, to the right. Aerofilms.

5. Edgware, 1926. Some signs of a new suburb emerge. Opposite the 1924 Underground terminus and its adjacent car depot are Leslie Raymond's Mall shops and flats approaching completion. To their right, preparations for a further extension of the railway are visible. George Cross's Premier Parade is still not quite finished.

66 *Later Extensions of the Original Underground System*

After the electrification of the original Metropolitan and District Railway in the 1903-6 their suburban expansion continued. In 1903 the District Railway began an electric service over a new line from Ealing to South Harrow but this did not prosper until the housing boom of the 1930s, when the Piccadilly Line deep level tube service was extended over it, giving direct access to the West End of London. In the same sector, in 1904, the Metropolitan Railway completed a branch from Harrow to the Middlesex town of Uxbridge, with a spur to meet the District at South Harrow which was used by District services to Uxbridge from 1910. Again the new electric services, running through open countryside some distance from the edge of London, were to see no significant suburban development until the building boom years of the late 1920s and the 1930s. Electrified branch lines opened by the Metropolitan railway, to Watford in 1925 and to Stanmore in 1932 enjoyed mixed fortunes. Although exploiting territory in which the housebuilders were active, the Stanmore branch saw much of its traffic drawn away to the Edgware tube line mentioned below by feeder buses and lower fares. Stanmore branch services also suffered from their edge-of-centre terminus in London (Baker Street) until Bakerloo line tube trains were projected over it in 1939.

The Metropolitan Railway, having started such diversification in 1881, took an even more active role in suburban development after 1919, forming a subsidiary company to exploit its surplus lands and buy other land alongside the line. New housing estates, ten in number by 1933, were then started in this "Metro-land". Avidly promoted by advertisements, brochures and booklets, they generated much remunerative traffic for the railway company.

To the east of London, District Railway electric trains were extended from Whitechapel to East Ham in 1905, serving late 19th century working class and lower middle class suburbs. These Underground trains, which ran over the existing London and Southend Railway after coming to the surface at Bow, reached Barking in 1908 and Upminster in 1932. With the 1932 extension, two Underground stations were opened in the vast London County Council Becontree housing estate, begun in 1920. Virtually a new town, by 1938 Becontree accommodated some 116,000, mostly in three to five room cottages and provided a great deal of traffic for the Under-

4

5

6. Entrance to Wood Green Station, on 23 April 1935. The electric tramcars are feeding in traffic from Palmers Green, Winchmore Hill and Enfield, to the north of the railway. Since they were both part of the same company, through tickets were available between points served by tube railway and tramways.

7. Golders Green station, looking towards Hendon and Edgware, November 1923. Traffic was not only fed into this station by the motor buses seen in the picture, but a whole new suburb had grown up around the station. The first section of an extension to Edgware, as far as Hendon, was just completed at the time this photograph was taken.

6

ground, not only in the rush hours. Other stations between Barking and Upminster were very soon busy with commuter traffic from private sector housing, much of it at the cheaper end of the market.

Tube Railway Suburbs

As with the first shallow subway Underground lines, the role of the deep level electrically-worked tube railways opened from 1890 onwards was initially one of *urban* transport, offering a faster alternative to vehicular traffic on the congested streets above.

But there was one exception. Ostensibly to reach cheap land for car sheds and sidings, the Charing Cross, Euston and Hampstead Railway was extended beyond Hampstead to emerge in the open at Golders Green, then a rural locality just beyond the edge of London. We say "ostensibly" because there is some suggestion that in planning this outer section, the promoters were involved, at one remove, in land syndicates. Opened in 1907, the Golders Green tube terminus certainly triggered very rapid development of a "green field" suburb. In the first full year of traffic this station handled 1.5 million passengers, but by 1915 the figure exceeded 10 million. A new shopping centre, a cinema, churches and over 4,100 houses were completed between 1905 and 1915. So intense was the building that when the railway was further extended in 1923 it had difficulty breaking out and some quite new houses had to be demolished.

The second era of tube railway development in London, from 1915 to 1940, saw some modification in the original concept of the deep level tube lines as urban rapid transit. What now developed was more complex. Whether this change in the original role was unwise is certainly arguable, but it was justified at the time on the grounds that cheaply-built suburban surface extensions would bring more traffic to the capital-intensive deep tunnel system, then operating below capacity. The process was begun in 1915-7 with the projection of Bakerloo tube trains on the surface alongside an existing trunk railway line as far as Watford, some 30 km north west from the centre, passing through areas largely undeveloped.

Other surface extensions followed, almost all through open countryside: from Wood Lane (White City) to Ealing in 1920; from Golders Green to Edgware in 1923-4; and from Finsbury Park to Southgate and Cockfosters in 1932-3. Also in 1932-3, tube services were projected over the earlier lines to South Harrow, Uxbridge and Hounslow. All this was in north

7

west and north London, which was to become the principal suburban territory exploited by the Underground.

Only one tube railway probed any distance through the difficult subsoils south of the river Thames, where the leading contender for suburban traffic was the Southern Railway, a conventional main line system, which had successfully electrified almost the whole of its suburban network by 1932. The new tube railway was in fact the pioneer deep level line in 1890, modernised and extended south to a surface terminus at Morden in 1926. All other stations on the new section were underground, in earlier suburbs which had grown with the help of street tramways and buses and to a lesser extent, conventional railways.

South of the Morden terminus lay open countryside. Here the arrival of the tube did much to stimulate rapid suburban growth between 1926 and 1939. This isolated sector of "Underground suburbia" prospered in part because it was not conveniently served by the Southern Railway but principally because the Underground Co and its successor London Transport, as operators of the main motor bus network, were able to establish new road services to bring in traffic from a wide area.

This integration of transport modes was so successful that very soon tube trains leaving Morden in the morning rush hours were so crowded with commuters from new housing that passengers at stations nearer London were complaining of difficulty in boarding.

With equal potency, in north and north west London the new tube extensions were encouraging development of commuter housing around their stations. Sometimes there was a slow start, but in every case almost the whole of the catchment areas had become fully built over by 1940.

The final stage of suburban tube railway expansion before World War Two was the 1935-40 London Transport New Works Programme, launched with Government financial assistance to stimulate employment in the depressed areas of heavy industry. Very soon rearmament began to slow progress and wartime contingencies brought the new works to a complete stop in 1940-1. Some unfinished sections were completed after 1945, but those extending into the new Green Belt were cancelled, even to the extent of abandoning partially-constructed engineering works. The scheme had included only two lengths of new suburban tube railway, one, north of Edgware, became a casual-

8

ty of the Green Belt cancellations, the other, a new tunnel link between two suburban steam railways in the eastern suburbs (Leytonstone to north Ilford at Newbury Park) was opened in 1947. The main thrust of the New Works Programme was to extend tube services into suburban areas over or alongside existing steam railways, replacing unattractive steam-hauled suburban trains serving established suburbs. The advantages of electrification were supplemented by greater convenience for the commuter, who would be carried directly into the central area Underground network instead of having to change to bus or Underground at main line termini remote from workplaces.

Perceptions and Reality

There can be no doubt that new suburbs served by the Underground were seen by potential commuters as superior to all others. This arose from a widespread perception of the Underground as modern, speedy, cheap, efficient and clean transport, offering an uninterrupted direct journey to central London workplaces, as well as affording the whole family ready access to large shopping, entertainment and sports centres in the inner area.

Its new suburban stations were inspiring examples of contemporary architecture, carefully designed to ease passenger flow, attractively illuminated after dark, and inviting and pleasant to use. They were adornments to the new suburbs and usually the only outstantding architecture in them.

Above all, Underground services were so frequent – timetables were not required by the user. Even outside the rush hours, suburban Underground stations offered trains every 5-12 minutes in contrast to the 20 minute or half-hourly intervals on other suburban lines, a discrepancy which still exists today. And travel was not only cheap but fully integrated; if a bus or street tramcar had to be taken to reach the Underground station, a combined fare and ticket was usually available.

All this was well promulgated by clever publicity, in a continuous stream of well-designed leaflets, booklets, posters and advertisements.

It was of course too good to be true: the reality was not always in line with the perception. Journeys into the suburbs on the often over-extended Underground services could be highly tedious since, unlike many suburban services on the conventional railways, the trains usually called at all the many closely-spaced stations.

9

10

8. Hendon Central Station under construction in what are still completely rural surroundings, 6 September 1923, looking east. This area was very soon to become a suburban commercial centre with shopping parades and apartments above, and a large cinema.

9. Hendon Central Station under construction, 10 August 1923, looking south towards London. Major earthworks have been completed, a road overbridge constructed and the station building (right) is almost finished.

10. Final touches being added to Hendon Central Station on 11 August 1924. At this point the line passes below some higher ground in separate tube tunnels. The signal box, with its tiled and hipped roof, reflects the architectural treatment of the main station buildings on this suburban extension.

11. F. Taylor, *New Works*, 1925. The Hampstead Tube was extended overground from Golders Green to Edgware in 1923-4, prompting new development in what had been open countryside around every station. A brand new tube station appears at the centre of a bustling suburban building site.

Underground trains, designed for urban traffic, also offered fewer seats and became unpleasantly overcrowded inside the central area. At speed, they were rough riding, whilst running noise, especially in tunnels, was often so overpowering that conversation was all but impossible. Most of these disadvantages remain for the suburban traveller today.

Scale of Suburban Operations

Although no satisfactory sequence of statistics is available, some idea of the scale of Underground suburban traffic and its growth can be indicated in what has to be a rather crude comparison. In 1902, around 410,500 persons were entering central London daily by rail between 5.00 and 10.30; of these, just over 76,000 were on Underground trains. By 1952, with wartime distorsions out of the way, before car commuting had assumed significant levels, and before the steep decline in central London jobs, it was estimated that of about two million people entering central London daily, 600,000 travelled by the Underground railways, 580,000 by conventional railways and the remainder by buses and private cars.

Egdware: The Underground Suburb. A Case Study

To consider the relationship between the Underground and suburban development in a little more detail, we may look at events in Edgware. This was a small village on the Roman Watling Street, about 15 km north west of the centre of London, with under 2,000 inhabitants in 1901, served by a single line branch railway offering a circuitous journey of 50 minutes to the City of London.

Cultivation of hay for London's vast army of horses was the principal occupation.

Some slight suburban growth followed the opening of an electric street tramway in 1904 but the trams did not provide direct access to central London, nor did the motor buses which appeared in 1913.

This early suburban development was also prompted by firm proposals to extend the tube railway from Golders Green to Edgware, for which some land had been purchased just before 1914. With a declining market for forage, it was apparent there would be no shortage of building land.

In 1921, the war over, a Government concerned by the high level of unemployment offered guarantees of interest and capital for schemes which would relieve it. One successful candidate was the surface extension of the tube railway from Golders Green to Edgware via Hendon. When construction began in 1922, land speculation intensified and an old lady

11

12. Cover of Metro-land booklet, published by the Metropolitan Railway, 1920s.

12

13. Artist unknown, *Into the Clean Air and Sunshine of Golders Green*, 1911.

70 occupying a house and a 2.02 hectare estate immediately opposite the site of the proposed tube terminus was finally persuaded to move out when offered over seven times the sum she had paid for it in 1919.

The new station, with a handsome frontage described as "Italian in style", was opened in August 1924. Its trains ran every 8 minutes at peak hours, every 10 minutes at other times, direct to central London in 35 minutes, entering the deep level tube system at Golders Green. At first the building stood almost isolated in open countryside apart from a row of new shops nearby.

The Underground Company soon began to arrange feeder motor bus services to bring in traffic from surrounding districts and, having learned a hard lesson at Golders Green, took steps to protect a path for a possible further extension of the railway.

In these early years, with land exchanging hands at up to ten times its agricultural value, there was more interest in trading land than building houses. In one year alone, that following the arrival of the railway, land values increased by 30-40%.

This speculation had an effect on the house prices, slowing sales, and consequently the traffic on the new Underground services proved disappointing.

The Underground Company, which although responsible for the increment in land values, received no share of it, complained in 1927 of a mere 14% growth in passenger numbers since the opening of the line.

Things began to improve as the 1920s ended. More houses were being built and the lane past the new station was widened to 27.4 metres between frontages, providing a fine new shopping street to form the centre of the new suburb. In 1929 the number of passengers using the station monthly had grown from the 1924 total of 75,000 to 233,000.

By 1931 trains were leaving Edgware every 2-3 minutes in the peak hours, every 5 at other times. A large Railway Hotel was completed that year and in 1932 a 2,120 seat cinema opened its doors. Both buildings were near the Underground station, adding strength to the new suburban centre.

The 1931 census showed the population to be almost 13,000, four times the 1921 figure.

As the 1930s advanced, the pace of house-building accelerated, large construction firms arrived and slightly cheaper houses became available. Police, postal, telephone, hospital, education and fire services were all expanded and social organisations were formed.

13

14. C. Sarland, *Light, Power and Speed*, 1910.

By 1939 the new suburb was complete. Most of its earning adults were travelling by Underground to work in central London and the railway was carrying about 24 million passengers annually between Golders Green and Edgware, principally in the peak hours. Work on a further extension, to Bushey Heath, and a relief line via Mill Hill and Finchley had begun.

Although as we have seen, post-war decisions would arrest further development, Edgware as a suburb brought to life and maturity by the Underground, was indisputably a success.

The Metropolitan Infrastructure in The New Millennium

"Much has been written about exploring the remotest corners of the earth, and probing the vast depths of space, but what of the world beneath our feet?" (The Author, *London's Underworld*, 1969)

And what of the future? The future of London's infrastructure. It is at the subterranean levels that the regeneration of London is beginning involving principally the statutory authorities and the transport undertakings – British Rail and London Transport together, of course. With the 33 local authorities (including the Corporation of London) and the London office of the Department of the Environment a mixture of public and private development below as well as above the surface of the capital is shaping the future of London in the next millennium. London and South East England was separated from the mainland of Europe about 8,000 years ago with the broaching of the "English Channel" – then an arm of the Atlantic Ocean – into the three quarters enclosed North Sea/Lake. The construction of the Channel Tunnel has as it were re-linked the British Isles with the European mainland – with the London-Paris railway axis providing a new impetus to regeneration of the two cities' infrastructures. ("A Tale of Two Under-Cities"?)

To bring about a new London ready for the new millennium – central, local and "statutory" government will have to:

1) Map/suvey the principal features of London beneath the surface – to follow up the new studies of the geological survey (the locus project) with a combined effort to assemble, assimilate all data relating to services below the surface as well as data from all major developments (in particular high rise office and tower blocks) with significant piles and foundations.

2) Introduce the concept of 3/4D planning in local authority considerations e.g. to examine the potential and possibilities of developments – large and small – below the surface e.g. shopping centres, office block levels, college, university levels, restaurants, sorting offices (post office), cinemas and places of amusement – thus releasing space on the surface for more parks, gardens and open spaces generally.

3) To organize exhibitions for all comprehensive developments revealing not only the visible implications of such development – but also their invisible infrastructural dimension – with the statutory undertaking as well as the local authorities and development having space to tell their story.

4) To encourage the organic development of vertical as well as horizontal zoning for industrial, residential and transport and service developments. It is along these lines that London, Paris, Rome, Madrid and all the capital cities of Europe will find a converging philosophy where space and people are "seen in the round" – in a three dimensional organic unity – a type of metropolitan gala in a healthy environment. Such is the shape of a progressive future for a London in its European setting, a London that is not "first among equals", but a first in an equality of difference.

5) To create a multi-disciplinary infrastructure culture across the length and breadth of Europe based on old universities and the central and local institutions that govern our capital cities.

Perhaps the most interesting development has been the first moves – which have taken a quarter of a century to materialize – to set up a European based Msc City Infrastructure Management Course at the University of East London in collaboration with 1) the Chalmers Institute of Technology (Göteborg) – Sweden; 2) the Aristotle University (Thessaloniki) – Greece; 3) the Technical University (Delft) – Holland; and 4) the University Polytechnic of Catalonia (Barcelona) – Spain. This will take place in September 1996, and will provide the framework for first multi-disciplinary courses to serve the needs of all those engaged in "managing" city foundations.

Ellis Hillman

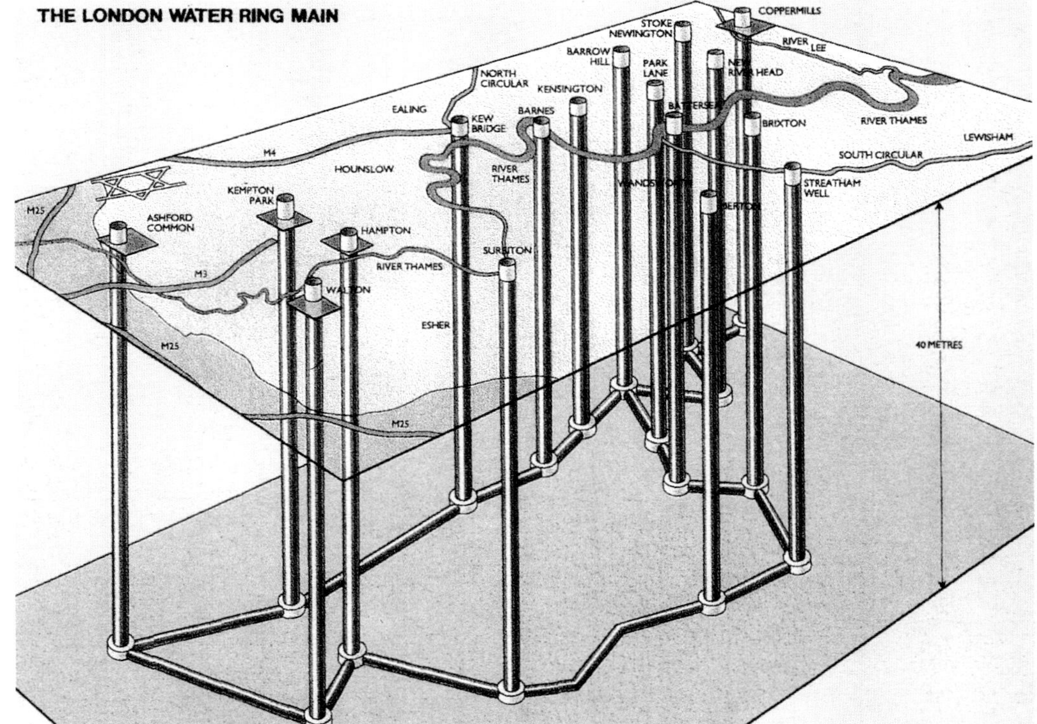

1. Map of the London Water Ring Main. Courtesy of Thames Water.

News from the companies

TrendPlus

The Esprit elevator at Saiedue 1996
Sabiem

74

Saiedue 1996 has staged a special, highly successful event: "Trend Plus", an exhibition-project on technological developments in the fields of architecture and interior design. Aimed at proposing new horizons for homes and constructions in general, "Trend Plus" (which presented more than 40 prestigious companies in a stand measuring a thousand square metres) was conceived like a great sign, conveying the role of the participating companies and emphasizing the chief characteristics of the exhibits.

In fact, as a by-product of the rapid diffusion of new systems of global communication, which change everyday habits and life styles, we feel a strong need to live in natural, comfortable environments characterized by low energy consumption.

This trend is reflected by the design of interiors and technological installations like lifts, both in homes and on public premises.
The interiors recreated in "Trend Plus" anticipate the styles and orientations of the future; the colours, materials, sounds and internal microclimates provide the different areas with a distinct identity. The relaxing hues of the office contrast with the warmer hues used

MOSTRA PROGETTO
SULLE TENDENZE E L'INNOVAZIONE TECNOLOGICA
NELL'ARCHITETTURA E NELLE FINITURE D'INTERNI

MOSTRA PROMOSSA ed
ORGANIZZATA DA
O N ORGANIZZAZIONE NIKE
su progetto
ORIGINAL DESIGNERS 6R5
DIVISIONE ARCHITETTURA
arch. ALBINO POZZI
FRANCESCO ROGGERO
Responsabile Segreteria LUISA CASADIO
Coordinamento LUCA ALBERGHINI

PARTNER UFFICIALI

ABET LAMINATI
AETAS
ALBANI & FONTANOT
ALDES
ARMSTRONG
ARQUATI
BIANCHI LEGNO
BPB ITALIA PLACO VIC
REGHERS
BTICINO
COREN
DIERRE
EFFE ITALIA
FIORENZA VETRAMREDO
FORBO RESILIENTI
FUSITAL
I C S A
JOTA BIOFA
JUNCKERS
LA FORTEZZA SUD
MAPEI
MARAZZI MARMO
MARAZZI TECNICA
MATI PIANTE PISTOIA
METEORA
ORKOS
PIAZZETTA
PL
PREFE
RASSENO
RIMADESIO
SAINT GOBAIN
SABIEM
SCHUNO
SICIS INTERNATIONAL
SIRI
TECHNOLUME
TRE PIU'
TRE P
VALLI & VALLI

in the home, while the hotel interior vaunts elegant, sophisticated colours. The materials have been chosen on the basis of several criteria; some are characterized by their original surface treatments, while others combat indoor pollution through the use of natural components. Isolating materials and ergonomic illumination contribute to render the interior serene.

The Esprit cabin meets all these requirements, and demonstrates the strong innovative aspects of its design, developed by Sabiem with Giugiaro Design.
The special "liquid textile" paints, the harmonious elliptic design of the control panel and the mirror, the soft visual effects created by the curved walls all reflect the design philosophy of the "Trend Plus" exhibition, representing a frame of reference for architects and for those visiting the fair.

Massimiliano Colombo

MEG Print hpl

The new operational centre
of Farmaceutica Rinaldi
Abet Laminati

Farmaceutica Rinaldi, who have operated for years in the town of Udine in the pharmaceutical materials distribution sector, have built their new plant in the Annonaria Zone in Udine, in an area situated immediately to the west of the main road axis.

The Udine Annonaria Zone is very well connected with the town and with the local and regional road systems, and the major companies operating in the distribution sector are already located there; it therefore guarantees that Farmaceutica Rinaldi's activities have the links that are essential to facilitate the arrival of supplies and a fast and efficient delivery service to customers.

The new complex of buildings housing this activity, realized entirely using prefabricated reinforced concrete supporting structures, roof coverings and infillings, is composed substantially of three zones, each for a different specific use, located in three adjoining but structurally distinct parts of the building.

- The offices, placed at the eastern end of the area, are structured over two floors above ground, in a construction that is closed off on the east side by an aluminium structural façade; this is partly transparent and openable, with double-glazing-type double glass mirrors, and partly fixed and blind, with insulated mirrors made up of MEG plates by Print. This latter material is used to cover the heads of the office volume and most of the south façade of the warehouse, so as to guarantee, by forming an insulated and ventilated façade, that energy consumption is kept down and – considering the use made of the complex – a high degree of protection against radiation in the summer. Beneath the floors used as offices is a floor below ground, used to house the archive and the system control rooms.

- The employees' entrance, changing rooms and toilet facilities form the connection between the office volume and the warehouse; these spaces develop over a single floor, even though a space has been found in part of this for a small room to enable the security personnel to rest.

- The main part of the complex consists of the pharmaceutical materials warehouse and the automated and automatable lines used for "picking"; that is, for the preparation of orders destined for the various chemists'.

The warehouse, in turn, is served by an area used for arrivals of supplies in large lorries and by one for departures, which take place in small vans. This part is characterized above all by the way in which the picking and mechanized handling of the items is dealt with in it, thanks

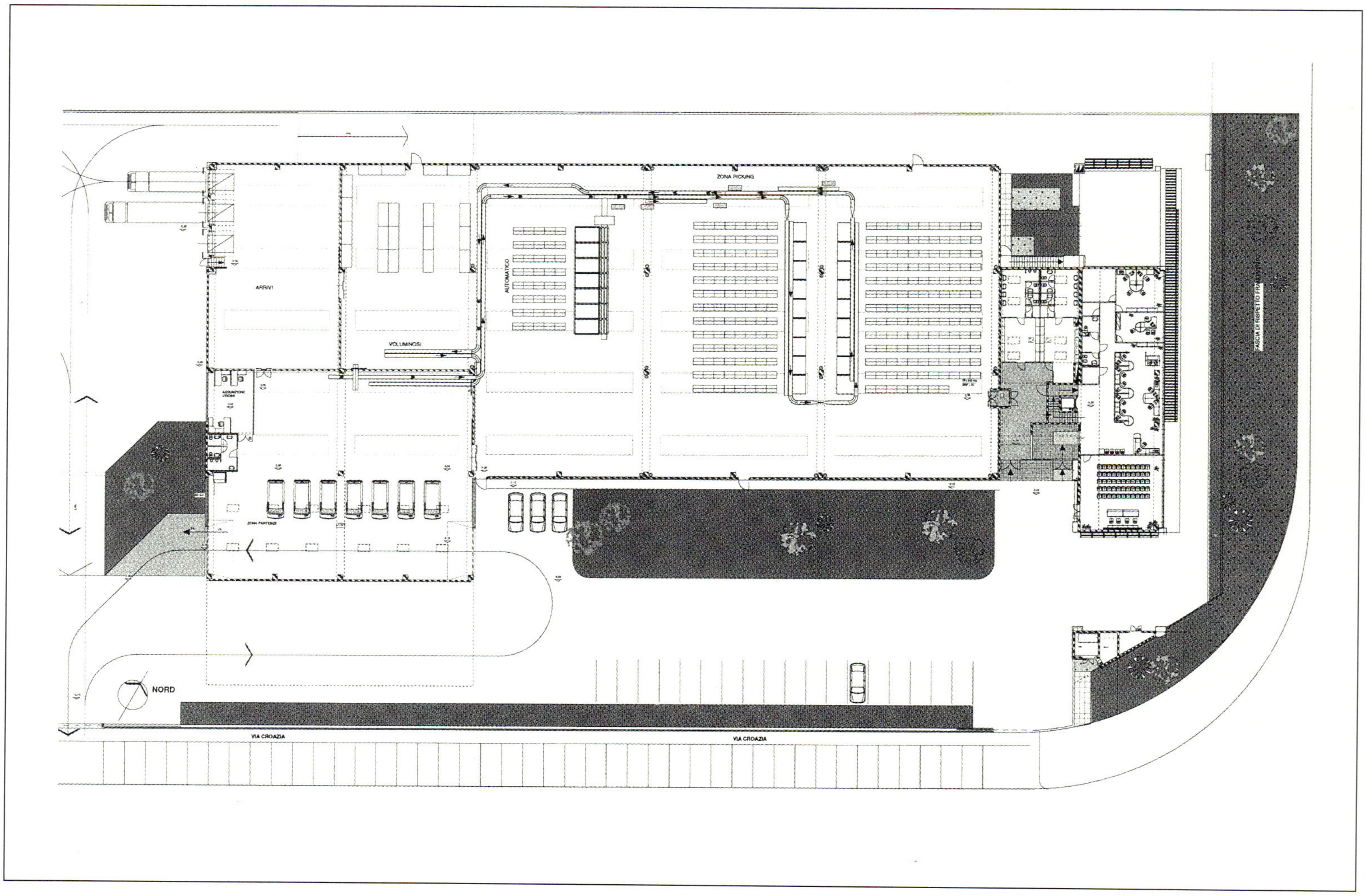

to highly modern systems which, with direct
and automated electronic links with client
companies, can perform extremely complex
functions in double-quick time.
Because of the function it performs, the shell
of this part of the building requires a high level
of performance; the MEG plates by Print, which,
as well as the volumes already described, also
cover the south façade of the warehouse,
take on an essential role here by guaranteeing
the reduction of summer heat gain through
the formation of a ventilated wall. A similar device
has been used for the roof cover, protected with
washed cement slabs, air chamber, impermeable
cladding and very thick insulating layer in the flat
parts and with an insulated sandwich of fretted
aluminium plates with ventilated cavities in the
sloping parts in a micro shed formation.
In addition to these "passive" devices there is a
sophisticated and powerful climatization system
which, together with the former, guarantees
that the appropriate temperature for storing the
materials in the warehouse is maintained.
To complete the complex, the ENEL
transformation and delivery box has been
realized near the pedestrian entrance to the
offices, and the company personnel can gain
direct access to this.
Joined to this small volume is a vertical element
acting as a support for the external lighting
for the service areas; in its shape and size,
this echoes the identical element that houses
the flues on the opposite side.

Project:
Parmegiani Giacomuzzi Moore Associati
Engineer Giuliano Parmegiani, Architect Lorenzo
Giacomuzzi Moore.

Plant Design:
TE.S.I. srl
Tecnologie e Servizi per l'Impiantistica.

Structural Calculations:
Engineer Antonio Battistella.

Construction:
Impresa Tobia Clocchiatti spa
Tesi System srl
Isalf
Conditerm srl
Claudio Tonutti - Impianti Elettrici.

Pab

Design by Studio Kairos
B&B Italia

photos by Studio Casanova

Pab is based on a very simple idea: a long sheet folded in half and supported by light weight braces that resemble lines. The resulting structure is a shelf unit that can be stacked or set side by side and is in itself a simple element of decoration.

Other elements include glass panels that protect shelves or storage areas, cabinet space for storing small objects, and thick benches that contrast with the narrow shelves. These elements, that come in different colours and sizes, can be mixed and matched to create a variety of combinations.

The shelf, the basic element of the Pab System, the fruit of a complex research of materials and technology, is synonymous with minimalism, simplicity, elegance, high-quality details, ecology. Thanks to the combination of different materials like birch and aluminium, the Pab System is suited to a wide range of categories of interiors. The shelves are also available in a version

featuring corner elements in aluminium. In addition to the shelves Pab, which vaunts an evident Functionalist heritage, comprises uprights in satiny-painted wood supporting CD holders, versatile benches in birch trees and a simple, large shelf which can be used for a television set or stereo equipment.

The discrete, non-obtrusive quality of the system, which avoids any undue interference with the life of its users, has been respected in the design of the container element, which consists of a simple screen in the form of a door in opalescent glass covering the space between the shelves, concealing an area which can be equipped with glass shelves or drawers. Along with the other elements, these containers with hinged doors or drawers in birch create a coherent, contemporary aggregate which can be summarized in the words aesthetic simplicity, practicality and accessibility, at the same time vaunting a distinct identity.

3D Bank

A new system for bank interiors
Castelli

Managerial 3D.

Companies operating in the field of furniture for offices and public premises must consider a large variety of aspects when conceiving their products: design, innovation and functionality. The latter is the sum of ergonomics, new technologies and a careful analysis of the evolution of office work. In particular, the banking sector has undergone radical changes; paper money is gradually being abandoned in favour of magnetic currency, and traditional bank deposits is, as a form of saving, being replaced by investment management. The banks must meet the demands of a changing market and a public in search for new products and services. As a result, the interior of banks must change radically, undergoing a true revolution which will not only involve the introduction of new technologies, but also the reorganization of the premises.

Aware of this situation, Castelli has developed the 3D Bank, a system designed on the basis of these concepts.

Along with the traditional counter we find easily recognizable work stations where the clients

Counter box - 3D Bank.

can receive consulting, reserved meeting rooms and comfortable waiting areas. When planning the layout, the arrangement of the furniture will be studied on the basis of the structural limits, to design an ideal path enabling the client to easily identify all facilities, from self service computer services to the traditional counter and the consulting area.

Thanks to the simple arrangement of the 3D Bank it is therefore possible to create tailor-made, versatile interiors that can easily be adapted to the needs of the clients or to new technologies. Moreover, the wide range of finishings allows the designer to "create" his own furniture system, without unnecessary restrictions.

Consulting area - 3D Bank.

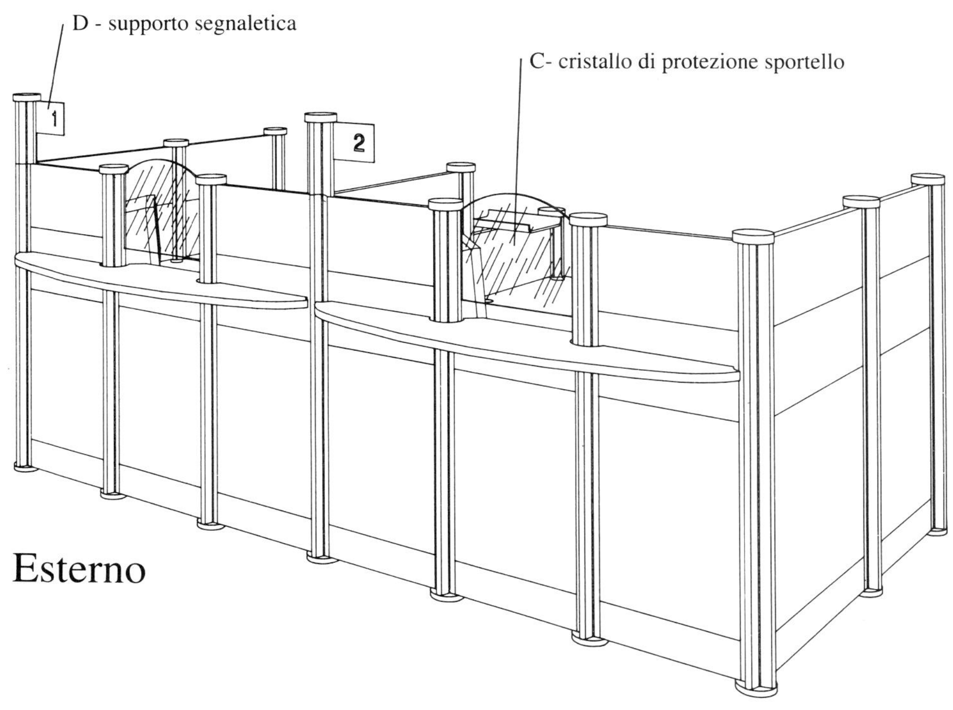

D - supporto segnaletica
1
2
C- cristallo di protezione sportello
Esterno

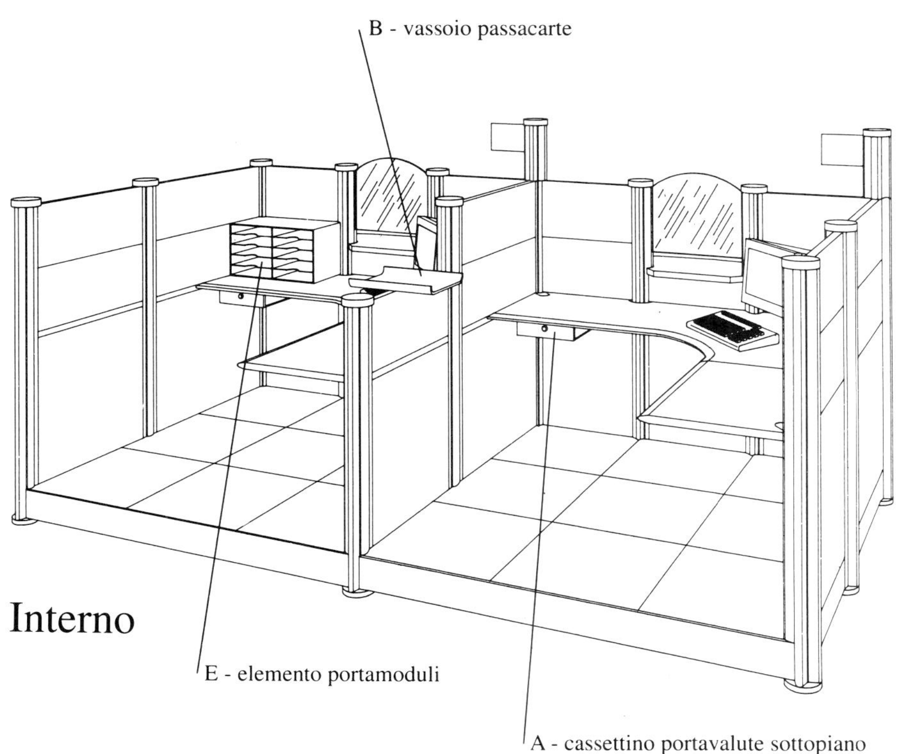

B - vassoio passacarte
Interno
E - elemento portamoduli
A - cassettino portavalute sottopiano

The Changes of the Home

Chiosco
Furniture series by Luca Meda
Molteni & C.

Fashion. Come on, for the love that leads to the seven deadly sins, stop for a moment and look at me.

Death. I'm looking at you.

Fashion. Don't you recognize me?

Death. You must know that I do not see very well, and that I cannot use glasses, because the English do not make any that suit me, and even if they did, I would not have any place to mount them.

Fashion. I am Fashion, your sister.

Death. My sister?

Fashion. Yes: don't you remember we were both borne from Transience?

Death. You must remember I am the mortal enemy of memory.

Fashion. But I remember it clearly; and I know that both of us tend to continuously undo and change things here on earth, only that you attain your goal in one way, and I in another.

Death. Unless you are talking to yourself or to someone inside your throat, speak louder and more clearly; if you continue muttering with that cobweb voice I will not understand you; you know that my hearing is no better than my sight.

Fashion. Even if it is not polite, and if in France one does not speak in order to be heard, I will do as you say, just because we are sisters and we cannot be overly respectful to one another. I say that our common nature and manner is to continuously renew the world, but you have from the beginning pounced on the persons and the blood; I am quite happy with beards and hair, clothes, furniture and buildings and such things. [...] If we were to compete in a race I do not know who of us would win, because if you run, I prefer galloping...

Fashion therefore gallops unrestrainedly, with fickle and unpredictable steps, continuously disrupting and overturning things. In his "moral operetta" Leopardi relates it to mother Transience and sister Death, describing it as a great power capable of undermining even the most stable and ancient of things. Thus it involves even "furniture" and "palaces", the façades of houses and their interiors, fittings and forms. And doing so, it captures them in an eternal and ephemeral pursuit of events and tastes. This is the point: how can the house adapt itself to the passing of time, to the advance and sudden changes of life, without falling into the vices of fashion, with its fugacity, its play on external appearances? A reply may perhaps come from the decision to enable the furniture to change its disposition and image within certain limits, both from day to day and throughout their existence, on the basis of their "theatrical" nature. This theatricality is part of their intrinsic character, of their role as sets and background: in fact, they represent the domestic "stage", the scenario against which the events of

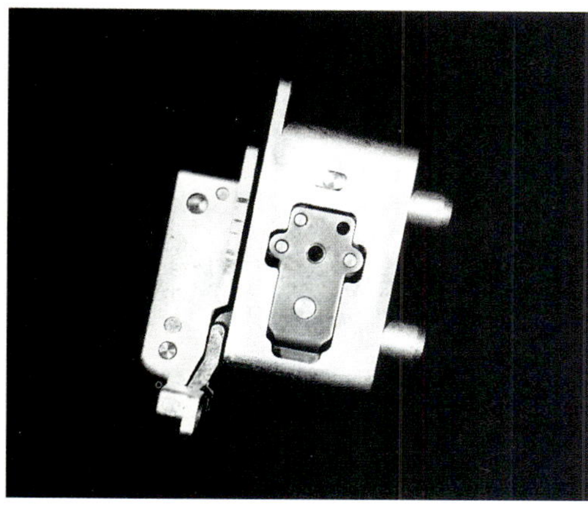 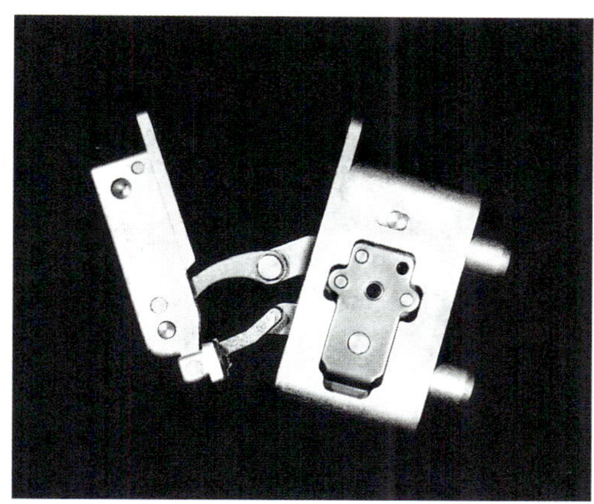 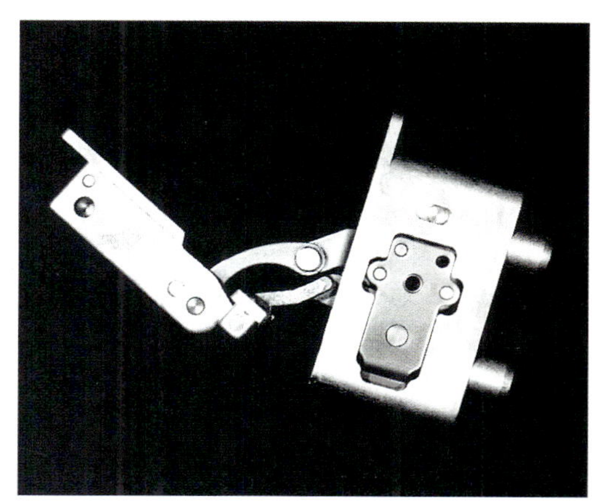

everyday life take place. This possibility to adapt the furniture to the circumstances both refers to its disposition and reciprocal superimposition in the interior and to the capacity to accommodate persons and gestures, their versatility in meeting changing requirements. This "art" is possible thanks to new technical developments and to the advanced level of technologies currently applied in the field of furniture manufacturing. Sigfried Giedion, the greatest writer of the modern vicissitude, saw the future of the home in the sense that "mechanisation takes command", as witnessed by the title of his famous book. We do not believe in this general myth, but rather in a new, more subtle system of possibilities guaranteed by the materials, devices, movements and combinations. A versatility which does not betray the formal stability and the tradition of the home.

Daniele Vitale

Chiosco

"I want a red pavilion with gilded minarets, / and slender alabaster columns..." (Théophile Gautier) Chiosco is a series of coordinated pieces of furniture conceived for the areas of the home that serve a public and representative purpose. It consists of furniture designed to show and contain, with closed or half-open glass doors, related to the sideboard or the bookcase, the chest or the showcase. But these units are accompanied by open structures, wooden backdrops hung on the wall, furrowed by slender cuts, capable of supporting shelves and drawers without visible joints or tension bars. Shelves mounted on hinges, which can be opened and closed as necessary, are also available: when they are not needed they merge discreetly with the wall. These "sets" support without being ostentatious, acting like small "theatre stages" evidencing what is placed before them. Low furniture or benches may, for instance, be placed in front of them, to accommodate the television, radio, computer or stereo. The range also includes complementary furniture, as dining tables and chairs, writing desks, small chests of drawers, clocks, consoles, small decorative tables and items in which to protect and show objects: a wide choice of pieces forming a general proposal for the home. Chiosco is based on the formal principle of distinguishing interior from exterior, and vertical elements from horizontal ones: the vertical structures are in pear wood, while the shelves are lacquered in a delicate ivory shade. It thus plays on a harmonious relationship between untreated materials and neat finishing treatments. The single parts of Chiosco are highly sophisticated. Hinges, skids, pistons, carriages and other mechanical devices are small and concealed, at times as tiny, precious details and, at times as embedded, invisible joints. And the movements are characterized by the rigor of geometric precision.

Dove trovare Rassegna

Librerie

- **Asolo**
  Libreria Polo Cart.
- **Bari**
  Libreria Feltrinelli
- **Bologna**
  Libreria Feltrinelli
  Libreria Il Leonardo
- **Bolzano**
  Libreria K.O. libri
- **Catania**
  Libreria de Martiniis
- **Cividale del Friuli**
  Libreria Muner G.
- **Como**
  Ass. culturale
- **Conegliano**
  Quartiere Latino Libri
- **Ferrara**
  Libreria Feltrinelli
  Architecnica
- **Firenze**
  Coop. libraria universitaria
  Coop. Un. Studio Lavoro
  Libreria Alfani
  Libreria Centro d'Arte Spazio Tempo
  Libreria Feltrinelli
  Libreria Lef
  Libreria Marzocco
- **Genova**
  Libreria Feltrinelli
- **Livorno**
  Libreria Belforte
- **Mestre**
  Libreria Don Chisciotte
- **Milano**
  Libreria Cortina
  Libreria CLUP
  Libreria Cusl
  Libreria Feltrinelli (Baires)
  Libreria Feltrinelli (Europa)
  Libreria Feltrinelli (Manzoni)
  Libreria Hoepli
  Libreria L'Archivolto
  Libreria M. Sedis (C.so Garibaldi)
  Libreria M. Sedis (Galleria)
  Libreria Unicopli

- **Modena**
  Libreria Feltrinelli
  Libreria M. Sedis
- **Napoli**
  Libreria CLEAN
  Libreria Guida
  Libreria Feltrinelli
  Libreria Il Punto
- **Padova**
  Libreria Feltrinelli
  Libreria Ginnasio
  Libreria Progetto
- **Palermo**
  Libreria Dante
  Libreria Feltrinelli
- **Parma**
  Libreria Feltrinelli
- **Pavia**
  La Libreria
- **Pescara**
  Libreria dell'Università
  Libreria Feltrinelli
  Libreria Filogrosso
- **Pisa**
  Libreria Feltrinelli
- **Pordenone**
  Libreria Al Segno
  Libreria Il Labirinto
  Libreria La Rivisteria
- **Ravenna**
  Libreria La Rinascita
- **Reggio Calabria**
  Libreria Pepo
- **Reggio Emilia**
  Libreria Vecchia Reggio
- **Roma**
  Libreria Dedalo
  Libreria Feltrinelli (Argentina)
  Libreria Feltrinelli (Babuino)
  Libreria Feltrinelli (Orlando)
  Libreria Kappa
  Libreria Rinascita
- **Rovereto**
  Coop. Libreria Rovereto

- **Salerno**
  Libreria Feltrinelli
- **Siena**
  Libreria Feltrinelli
- **Taranto**
  Libreria Dichens
- **Torino**
  Libreria Agorà
  Libreria Celid
  Libreria Comunardi
  Libreria Feltrinelli
  Libreria Internazionale Salone
- **Trento**
  La Rivisteria
  Libreria Universitaria
- **Treviso**
  Galleria del Librario
  Libreria Canova
  Libreria Marton
- **Trieste**
  Coop. Fra Servi
  Libreria Italo Svevo
  Libreria La Fenice
  Libreria Tergeste
- **Udine**
  Libreria Tarantola
- **Venezia**
  Libreria Arsenale
  Libreria Nuova Cluva
  Libreria Fantoni
- **Verona**
  Libreria Catullo
  Libreria Rinascita
- **Vicenza**
  Libreria Galla
  Libreria Spazio Più
  Libreria Traverso

- **Lugano**
  Libreria Melisa
- **Madrid**
  Xarait Libros

Distributori

Italia

- **Joo Distribuzione**
  Via F. Argelati 35, 20123 Milano
  tel. 02/8375671

- **Quadrifoglio Libri** (Tre Venezie)
  Via S. Breda 24/B, 35010 Limena, PD
  tel. 049/768099 - 8840276

Distribution

Worldwide

- **North America**
  Birkhäuser Boston
  c/o A.I.D.C.
  12, Winter Sport Lane
  Williston, VT 05495, USA
  tel. 802 862 0095, fax 802 864 7626
- **Germany**
  Birkhäuser Verlag AG
  c/o Springer-Verlag Berlin
  Postfach 311340
  D-10643 Berlin
  tel. 030/5207423, fax 030/8207448

- **Austria**
  Birkhäuser Verlag AG
  c/o Springer-Verlag Wien
  Sachsenplatz 4-6
  P.O. Box 89 A 1201 Wien
  tel. 01/33024 15/226 o. 266
  fax 01/33024 2662
- **All other countries:**
  Birkhäuser Verlag AG
  Postfach 250
  CH-4105 Biel-Benken
  tel. 41/61/7217784, fax 41/61/7217950

Dove non è possibile usare il legno, si può usare la sua bellezza.

Per questo c'è Parqcolor.

PARQCOLOR, il nuovo pavimento a doghe, inventato per non rinunciare alla bellezza del legno, è in laminato ad alta pressione prodotto in 44 splendidi decori legno.
RESISTE AD OGNI TIPO DI USURA.
Non richiede lamatura e verniciatura. Si installa senza bisogno di inchiodare o incollare con un semplice incastro di doghe, senza sollevare polvere. È prodotto con materiali puliti nel rispetto dell'ambiente.

nella foto: show room Welonda
Castiglione delle Stiviere (MN)
- pavimento realizzato
in Parqcolor faggio dogato 9226

PL spa
22070 Vertemate (CO)
Strada Prov.le per Bulgorello, 1
tel. 031/888.211 - fax 031/901.053
telex 380155 PL I

GRUPPO ABET

Per l'edilizia
c'è un grande
SAIE

"

FCL comunicazione

"

SAIE96

BOLOGNA
16-20 OTTOBRE 1996
Salone Internazionale dell'Industrializzazione Edilizia
International Building Exhibition

Fiere Internazionali di Bologna Ente Autonomo - Italia   Tel.051/282111 Fax 051/282332 - Internet: http://www.smart.it/SAIE

BolognaFiere

The complete collection of Rassegna magazine featuring architecture, design, and graphic arts. A continuous chronicle covering the history of modern design. Architects, cities, projects, interior design, furnishings, and exemplary moments of the Modern Movement, in a rigorous succession of treated themes, are meant to be a useful tool of consultation for information about the history of modern architecture. Editor: Vittorio Gregotti. Editorial office: via Matteo Bandello 20, 20123 Milano, telephone (2).4812448. Publisher: Cipia S.r.l., via Stalingrado 97/2, 40128 Bologna, telephone (51).327929. Publishing services: Editrice Compositori, via Stalingrado 97/2, 40128 Bologna, telephone (51).327811.

RASSEGNA

Next issues

67 (Airships)
edited by Sebastiano Brandolini

Dirigibles represent one of the most accomplished results of building technology applied to the problems of flight, both due to their refinement and their intelligent design. In the contest between the advocates of "lighter than air" and those in favour of heavier vehicles the dirigible was eventually defeated. In Italy the dirigible is associated with the name of Umberto Nobile, a genial constructor and the inventor of semi-rigid airships, very easy to steer, conceived as research and military vehicles. Ferdinand von Zeppelin launched the most significant commercial exploitation of dirigibles. Designed with a principally rigid and undeformable structure, Zeppelin dirigibles flied until 1937, when the tragedy of the *Hindenburg* dirigible marked their rapid disappearance. The interest in dirigibles is also associated with a development of design systems which we could place between industrial design and a very high level of craftsmanship. This applies both to the structure of the airship and to the groud structures, the hangars, which not only protected the flying machines but also guaranteed a completely safe take-off, and the design of special interiors and accessories.

68 (Anatole de Baudot)
edited by Marie-Jeanne Dumont

Student of H. Labrouste and E. Viollet-le-Duc, Anatole de Baudot is known to architecture history for the Saint-Jean church at Montmartre, in Paris, the first sacred building where reinforced concrete was used on a large scale. De Baudot opened the way to structural rationalism, avoiding compromises with the historical styles and basing his doctrine on the principle of unity of the constructive structure and on an architectural composition based on structural reasoning rather than on calculation.

69 (Great Machines)
edited by Franz A. Engler

The expression "great machine" evokes the idea of an object eliciting wonder, marvel, surprise by virtue of its complexity, visible or invisible, its unusual size, its function. In this century speaking of great machines means referring to cranes, radio and TV masts, ship elevators, excavators, *ponts transbordeurs*, parabolic telescopes, missile platforms or oil rigs, blast furnaces. Yet large dimensions lead, as a complementary and inevitable phenomenon, to the disappearance of the machines, either because they are hidden from sight (as for example with the Geneva particle accelerator), or because they are miniaturized, as happens with data transmission networks, transferring large dimensions onto other planes.
This issue of *Rassegna* illustrates each one of these great machines of the contemporary age, also with a certain attention devoted to the role these objects have played in the artistic imagination.

ORDER CARD

1. Subscription rate one year (4 issues)
   ☐ Lit. 156,000

2. Order back issue Lit. 49,000 each

   issue no. | quantity

3. Payment to **CIPIA** srl by:

   ☐ Bank cheque

   ☐ c/o Banca Popolare di Milano
   Ag. n. 4 - c/c n. 8943

   ☐ c/c postale n. 12879409,

Name and surname ________________________

Address ________________________

Zip code City and Country ________________________

☐ Credit Card   Amount ________________

☐ CartaSì   ☐ VISA   ☐ EuroCard   ☐ MasterCard

Card no. ________________ Expiry date ________

Birth date ________________

Date ________ Signature ________________

RASSEGNA

CIPIA s.r.l.
Via Stalingrado, 97/2°
40128 Bologna
I T A L Y

E D I T R I C E
COMPOSITORI

Trend Plus

L'ascenseur Esprit au Saiedue 1996
Sabiem

L'édition 1996 du Saiedue a concentré l'attention des visiteurs sur un événement particulier : "Trend Plus", une exposition réservée aux innovations technologiques réalisées en matière d'architecture et de finitions pour les espaces intérieurs.
Ayant pour objectif de suggérer de nouveaux horizons pour l'habitat et la construction, l'exposition "Trend Plus" (qui réunissait plus de 40 entreprises de grand renom en un même stand de mille mètres carrés) a créé un espace d'exposition conçu tel un grand signe, capable de lancer un message vibrant quant au rôle des participants et faire ressortir les caractères saillants des produits exposés.
En effet, face à l'affermissement rapide des nouveaux systèmes de communication globale qui changent les habitudes et les moeurs de la vie quotidienne, on assiste au renforcement du besoin de vivre dans un milieu naturel, confortable et à bas niveau de consommation d'énergie. Cette tendance se reflète sur les finitions des espaces intérieurs et sur des équipements technologiques comme l'ascenseur, tant dans les milieux domestiques que dans les endroits publics.
"Trend Plus" a construit des cadres s'inspirant des goûts et des tendances du futur, en utilisant des couleurs, des matériaux, des sons, des microclimats intérieurs permettant de caractériser la définition de différents espaces : des tons délassants pour le bureau, on passe aux teintes chaudes de la maison et aux couleurs élégantes et sophistiquées des hôtels.
Les matériaux adoptés suivent plusieurs conditions préalables : certains privilégient l'effet tactile, d'autres se proposent de s'opposer aux formes de pollution intérieures en recourant à des composants naturels. D'autre part, la qualité de l'habitat est améliorée par des matériaux qui assurent l'isolation acoustique et par l'utilisation ergonomique de la lumière.
Tous ces éléments se retrouvent dans l'ascenseur Esprit qui, inséré dans ce cadre, montre la grosse charge innovatrice du projet (conçu par Sabiem et Giugiaro Design).
Les pastels tendres de la cabine d'Esprit sont obtenus grâce à des peintures spéciales à "tissu liquide". Les lignes harmonieuses et elliptiques du tableau de commande et du miroir, la perception visuelle douce qui est créée par les parois à plan courbe se sont parfaitement intégrées dans la philosophie conceptuelle de "Trend Plus" et ont constitué un élément très attirant pour les architectes et les visiteurs du salon.

Massimiliano Colombo

MEG Print hpl

Le nouveau siège opérationnel
de Farmaceutici Rinaldi
Projet de Parmegiani Giacomuzzi Moore
Associati
Abet Laminati

La Sté Farmaceutica Rinaldi, qui a opéré pendant des années à Udine, dans le secteur de la distribution de matériel pharmaceutique, a réalisé le nouveau siège de ses activités dans le cadre de la Zone Annonaria Udinese, dans une arche située immédiatement à l'ouest du principal axe routier.
La Zone Annonaria Udinese est extrêmement bien reliée à la ville et au réseau routier local et régional. Il y existe déjà les principaux établissements opérant dans le secteur de la distribution. Elle offre donc à la Sté Farmaceutica Rinaldi les raccordements essentiels pour faciliter l'arrivée des fournitures et pour assurer un service de livraison à la clientèle rapide et efficace. Le nouveau complexe qui accueille cette activité a été entièrement construit avec des structures portantes, des couvertures et des façades préfabriquées en béton armé. Elle est essentiellement composée de trois zones d'utilisation spécifique qui se situent dans les trois parties de l'édifice, trois parties contiguës mais structurellement distinctes.
- Les bureaux sont situés dans la partie la plus à l'est de la zone et ils s'élèvent sur deux étages, dans un corps de fabrication fermé sur le côté est par une façade structurelle en aluminium, en partie transparente et s'ouvrant par des surfaces vitrées en double vitrage et formant une chambre de verre et, en partie, fixe et aveugle avec des surfaces vitrées isolées formées de plaques MEG Print. Ce matériel recouvre les têtes du corps des bureaux et une grande partie des façades sud du dépôt de manière à limiter, grâce à la formation d'une façade isolée et ventilée, la consommation d'énergie et – compte tenu du rôle du complexe – une forte protection contre l'ensoleillement estival.
Au-dessous des étages réservés aux bureaux, le sous-sol abrite les archives et les centrales des équipements.
- L'entrée des salariés, les vestiaires et les toilettes servent de trait d'union entre le corps des bureaux et le dépôt ; ces espaces ne se dressent que sur un étage, bien que l'on ait aménagé sur une partie de celui-ci, un minuscule logement permettant au personnel de gardiennage de se reposer.
- La partie principale du complexe est constituée par le dépôt de matériel pharmaceutique et par les lignes automatisées, ou pouvant l'être, destinées au *picking*, c'est-à-dire à la préparation des commandes destinées aux différentes pharmacies. Le dépôt est, à son tour, desservi par une zone réservée à l'arrivée des fournitures livrées par des poids lourds aux grandes dimensions et par une autre zone destinée aux départs qui sont assurés par des fourgons. Cette partie se caractérise surtout par la façon dont sont effectués – à l'intérieur – le *picking* et la manutention mécanisée des articles traités, avec des systèmes ultramodernes qui, en lien électronique direct et automatisé avec les clients, peuvent accomplir des fonctions extrêmement complexes dans des délais très rapides.
A cause de sa fonction, l'enveloppe de cette partie de l'édifice doit présenter des performances de haut niveau. Les plaques MEG de Print qui, en plus des tâches précédemment décrites, recouvrent la façade sud du dépôt, jouent ici un rôle essentiel pour garantir, grâce à l'existence d'une paroi ventilée, la réduction du gain thermique estival. Une mesure analogue a été adoptée pour la toiture qui est protégée par des plaques en ciment lavé, une chambre à air, une gaine imperméable et une couche isolante de forte épaisseur dans les parties plates et par un sandwich isolé de plaques grecques en aluminium, doté d'un espace vide ventilé, dans les parties inclinées pour former des micro-*sheds*.
Ces solutions "passives" sont complétées d'un système de climatisation sophistiqué et puissant qui, avec ces dernières, permet de maintenir une température constante appropriée à la conservation du matériel en stock.
A peu de distance de l'entrée des bureaux réservée aux piétons, on a bâti une centrale de transformation et de fourniture de courant électrique à laquelle peut accéder directement le personnel de l'entreprise.
Cette petite construction est liée à un élément vertical qui sert de support à l'éclairage extérieur des places. Par sa forme et ses dimensions, il répète l'élément qui, sur le côté opposé, abrite les carneaux montants.

Projet :
Parmegiani Giacomuzzi Moore Associati
Ing. Giuliano Parmegiani, Arch. Lorenzo Giacomuzzi Moore.

Projet des équipements :
TE.S.I. srl
Tecnologie e Servizi per l'Impiantistica.

Calculs structurels :
Ing. Antonio Battistella.

Réalisation :
Impresa Tobia Clocchiatti spa
Tesi System srl
Isalf
Conditerm srl
Claudio Tonutti – Impianti Elettrici.

Pab

Projet de Studio Kairos
B&B Italia

Pab se base sur une idée très simple : une longue feuille pliée au milieu et retenue par des légers tirants, qui semblent des signes. L'ensemble devient un superficie d'appui continue, qui peut être assemblée en longueur et en hauteur et qui est déjà suffisante pour définir des situations minimum d'ameublement.

Des panneaux en verre pour protéger les volumes ou les superficies, des compartiments pour ranger des petits objets, des bancs très épais qui contrastent avec les fines étagères, sont des autres éléments qui permettent, aussi bien grâce aux associations de couleurs qu'aux différentes dimensions, une articulation géométrique du système.

Elément de base du système Pab et résultat d'une élaboration complexe effectuée sur les matériaux et les moyens technologiques, l'étagère exprime un concept minimaliste, simple, élégant, écologique et une grande qualité des détails.

Grâce à l'utilisation de différents matériaux tels que le bouleau ou l'aluminium, le système Pab peut meubler différents habitats.

L'étagère peut avoir un élément d'angle en aluminium, comme finition des têtes.

D'un caractère franchement fonctionnel, Pab ajoute aux étagères des éléments de dossiers en bois peint satiné, servant de support aux porte-CD et aux porte-cassettes et des bancs en bouleau aux fonctions multiples, allant du simple, mais large, plan d'appui au plan prévu pour le téléviseur ou la chaîne hi-fi.

Pour ce qui est de la capacité que le système a de laisser vivre aussi l'espace vital – et de demeurer donc discret – on a résumé l'élément prévu pour le rangement en une simple armature constitué d'une porte en verre traité à l'acide qui coulisse entre les étagères et qui masque un volume pouvant accueillir des étagères en verre ou des tiroirs. Les espaces de rangement à porte basculante ou à tiroirs en bois de bouleau créent, avec les autres éléments du système, une relation au langage contemporain cohérente que l'on peut résumer ainsi : simplicité, commodité, facilité d'accès et identité précise.

3D Bank

Un système pour les nouvelles succursales de banque
Castelli

Les entreprises qui se consacrent à l'ameublement des bureaux ou des lieux publics doivent concevoir leurs produits en tenant compte des différents aspects qui composent un projet : le design, l'innovation et le fonctionnel. Ce dernier n'est que la résultante d'une équation donnée par l'ergonomie, l'étude de nouveaux moyens thermiques et l'analyse attentive du monde du travail. De façon plus particulière, le monde de la banque a subi d'importantes mutations dues aux exigences requises aujourd'hui par la gestion de l'argent. Le papier-monnaie perd du terrain face aux cartes magnétiques. Au niveau de l'épargne, le dépôt bancaire traditionnel est remplacé par la gestion des investissements. Les stratégies bancaires devront être plus attentives aux exigences d'un marché en pleine évolution et intéressé par des produits et des services nouveaux. Il en découle que l'aménagement des succursales de banque doit changer de façon radicale et entreprendre une véritable révolution qui conduira, non seulement, à l'adoption de nouveaux moyens technologiques, mais aussi, à l'intervention de l'organisation interne.

Castelli répond aux nouvelles exigences avec 3D Bank, un système conçu à la lumière de ces dernières. Le grand guichet traditionnel est accompagné de nouveaux aménagements destinés aux services conseil et repérés facilement par la clientèle, des zones consacrées aux réunions discrètes et de commodes espaces d'attente.

Pour l'élaboration de l'aménagement, la disposition des meubles est étudiée en partant des contraintes structurelles, de façon à tracer un parcours idéal grâce auquel le client pourra accéder facilement à tous les services, de la zone informatique en libre-service au guichet traditionnel et à la zone réservée au conseil.

La simplicité de la composition de 3D Bank permet aussi de mieux personnaliser les espaces qu'il sera facile de modifier, tant à cause des exigences de l'utilisateur que pour des raisons liées aux innovations technologiques, de façon à pouvoir toujours trouver la meilleure solution. Même au niveau de la forme, la multiplicité des finitions des éléments laisse au concepteur une large possibilité de créer soi-même son propre système d'aménagement, le libérant ainsi de bien des contraintes.

Les changements de la maison

Chiosco
Une série de meubles de Luca Meda
Molteni & C.

Mode. Allez, au nom de l'amour que tu as pour les sept péchés capitaux, arrête-toi de temps en temps et regarde-moi.

Mort. Je te regarde.

Mode. Tu ne me reconnais pas?

Mort. Tu devrais savoir que je n'ai pas une bonne vue et que je ne peux pas porter de lunettes, parce que les anglais n'en font pas qui m'aillent bien et que, même s'ils en faisaient, je ne saurais pas où les mettre.

Mode. Je suis la Mode, ta soeur.

Mort. Ma soeur?

Mode. Oui et ne te rappelles-tu pas que nous sommes nées toutes deux de la même Caducité?

Mort. Comment pourrais-je me rappeler, moi qui suis l'ennemie capitale de la mémoire?

Mode. Mais moi, je me le rappelle bien et je sais que, toutes les deux, nous jouons pareillement à défaire et à refaire continuellement les choses d'ici-bas, même si tu le fais à ta manière et moi, à la mienne.

Mort. A moins que tu ne parles à ta pensée ou sur le lobe de l'oreille de quelqu'un, élève un peu la voix et scande mieux tes mots ; si tu continues à me parler en grommelant entre tes dents, avec ta voix de moineau, je ne t'entendrai que demain car, si tu ne le sais pas encore, mon ouïe est aussi basse que ma vue.

Mode. Bien que ce soit contraire à la bonne éducation et qu'en France, on n'ait pas l'habitude de parler pour être entendus, comme nous sommes soeurs et qu'il est inutile de faire des compliments entre nous, je te parlerai comme tu veux. Je dis que notre nature et notre habitude commune nous amènent à rénover continuellement le monde, mais toi, tu t'es toujours jetée sur les hommes et sur le sang. Moi, je me contente, tout au plus, de la barbe et des cheveux, des vêtements, des meubles, des demeures et ainsi de suite. [...] Si nous devions nous mesurer au "palio", je ne sais qui remporterait la course, car si tu sais courir, je peux, quant à moi, galoper...

La mode galope donc éperdument sur le monde, à pas volages et imprévus, ne cessant de tout défaire et de tout bouleverser. Dans son "operetta morale", Leopardi l'apparente à Mère Fragilité et à Soeur Mort et il la décrit comme une énorme puissance capable de ronger les choses les plus stables et les plus anciennes. Ainsi, elle bouleverse l'ameublement et les palais, l'allure des maisons, les meubles et leurs formes. Les impliquant, elle les entraîne dans une poursuite éternelle et caduque d'affaires et de goûts. La question est bien là : comment la maison peut-elle s'adapter à la poursuite, à l'avancée et aux changements subits de la vie, sans pour autant tomber dans les vices de la mode, dans son caractère éphémère, dans son tourbillon d'apparences extérieures? Un embryon de choix naît peut-être du choix suivant : mettre les meubles en condition de changer, à l'intérieur de certaines limites, leur aspect et leur image, tant dans l'espace d'une journée que dans le cadre plus vaste de leur existence tout entière, à partir de leur nature "théâtrale". Ce caractère théâtral découle de leur nature intrinsèque en vertu de laquelle ils se présentent aussi bien comme coulisses que comme décor, car ils constituent la "scène" domestique, le milieu destiné à accueillir les affaires changeantes du quotidien. Cet art possible d' "adapter" les meubles aux circonstances concerne aussi bien la disposition des pièces, que les superpositions réciproques, la capacité d'accueillir des personnes et des gestes, la souplesse de répondre aux événements comme aux exigences. Cet "art" est permis par les niveaux moyens techniques, par le haut niveau de technologie que les meubles incorporent finalement. Sigfried Giedion, le plus grand narrateur de la vie moderne imaginait que dans le futur de la maison, "la mécanisation prendrait le commandement", comme le proclamait le titre de son célèbre ouvrage. Nous ne croyons plus aujourd'hui dans ce mythe générique ; nous lui préférons le système plus nouveau et plus subtil des possibilités qui sont offertes par les matériaux, les mécanismes, les mouvements et les combinaisons. Une capacité d'adaptation ne trahissant pas la stabilité de la forme et la tradition de la maison.

Daniele Vitale

Chiosco

"Je veux un kiosque rouge, aux minarets dorés, / Aux minces colonnes d'albâtre..." (Théophile Gautier)
Chiosco est une série de meubles coordonnés conçus pour les zones à caractère public et représentatif de la maison. Cette série se constitue tout d'abord de meubles faits pour montrer et contenir, vitrés fermés ou à demi fermés, liés au buffet ou à la bibliothèque, à la huche ou à la vitrine. Il existe également des structures ouvertes, des fonds en bois accrochés au mur et rainurés d'entailles minces, capables de soutenir des étagères et des chiffonniers sans supports visibles et sans tirants. Les étagères peuvent se transformer en battants à charnières, tantôt ouverts, tantôt fermés. Ce sont des fonds qui soutiennent avec légèreté mais qui se présentent aussi comme de petites "scènes théâtrales" donnant du relief à ce qui se trouve devant. Devant, on peut y mettre des meubles bas ou des bahuts destinés à accueillir de façon rationnelle le téléviseur et la radio, l'ordinateur ou la chaîne hi-fi. La série comprend également des meubles complémentaires comme des tables et des sièges pour les repas, des bureaux, de petits chiffonniers, des horloges, des consoles, des tables basses de service et de décoration, de petits meubles indépendants pour abriter et exposer des objets : une foule de pièces différentes, capables d'élaborer un aménagement général de la maison. Chiosco se base sur le principe de la distinction des espaces intérieurs et des extérieurs, des structures verticales et des plans horizontaux. Les structures verticales sont en bois de poirier ; les plans sont peints d'une délicate laque ivoire. La série joue donc sur les rapports harmoniques existant entre les matériaux bruts et sur la clarté des revêtements. Elle s'appuie sur des éléments et des pièces d'une grande finesse technique. Elle rapetisse et cache les mécanismes de mouvement, les charnières, les patins, les pistons et les coulisseaux ; elle en fait des objets menus et précieux, tantôt encastrés, tantôt cachés. Elle donne aux mouvements la rigueur de l'exactitude géométrique.

Trend Plus

Der Aufzug Esprit beim Saiedue 1996
Sabiem

Saiedue 1996 zog die Aufmerksamkeit der Besucher mit einem besonderen Ereignis auf sich: "Trend Plus", die Projektausstellung über die technologische Innovation in der Architektur und den Innenausarbeitungen. Mit dem Ziel, neue Horizonte des Wohnens und Konstruierens zu vermitteln, schuf die Ausstellung "Trend Plus" (die über 40 hervorragende Firmen in einem kollektiven Stand von tausend Quadratmetern vereinte) einen als großes Zeichen konzipierten Ausstellungsraum, der imstande war, eine starke Botschaft über die Rolle der teilnehmenden Firmen zu übermitteln und die wichtigsten Charakteristiken der ausgestellten Produkte zu erweitern.
Der raschen Ausbreitung neuer Systeme globaler Kommunikation gegenüber, die Gewohnheiten und Bräuche des täglichen Lebens verändern, bestätigt sich ja neuerlich das Bedürfnis, in einem natürlichen, komfortablen Ambiente mit geringem Energieverbrauch zu leben. Dieser Trend wirkt sich sowohl im häuslichen, als auch im kollektiven Rahmen auf die Innenausarbeitung und die technologischen Anlagen wie den Aufzug aus.
"Trend Plus" konstruierte Szenerien, welche zukünftige Geschmäcker und Orientierungen vorwegnehmen, wobei Farben, Materialien, Töne und interne Mikroklimas verwendet werden, um die Definition der verschiedenen Räume zu kennzeichnen; von entspannenden Farbtönen für das Büro gelangt man zu warmen Farben für das Heim und zu eleganten, raffinierten für das Hotel.
Die ausgewählten Materialien entsprechen mehreren Voraussetzungen: einige durch Privilegierung des Tasteffekts, andere durch Kontrastierung der Formen von *Indoor*-Verschmutzung mittels Verwendung von natürlichen Bestandteilen. Außerdem wird die Wohnqualität durch Materialien verbessert, die akustische Isolierung gewährleisten, sowie durch einen ergonomischen Einsatz des Lichts.
Alle diese Elemente finden ihre Bestätigung im Aufzug Esprit, der im Rahmen dieses Kontextes den starken innovativen Schwung seines Projekts (das von Sabiem mit Giugiaro Design entwickelt wurde) bewiesen hat. Die weichen, durch die speziellen Anstriche mit "flüssigem Stoff" erzielten Pastellfarben der Esprit-Kabine, die harmonischen ellipsenförmigen Linien der Druckknopfleiste und des Spiegels, sowie die von den Wänden mit gekrümmtem Grundriß geschaffene *softe* visuelle Perzeption fügten sich perfekt in die Projektsphilosophie der Schau "Trend Plus" ein und bildeten damit ein Element der Anziehung für die Architekten und die Besucher der Ausstellung.

Massimiliano Colombo

MEG Print hpl

Der neue Arbeitsfirmensitz
von Farmaceutici Rinaldi
Projekt von Parmegiani Giacomuzzi Moore
Associati
Abet Laminati

Farmaceutica Rinaldi spa, die in Udine jahrlang auf dem Gebiet des Pharmamaterialvertriebs tätig war, errichtete den neuen Sitz für ihre Aktivitäten im Rahmen des Ernährungsamtsgebiets von Udine auf einem unmittelbar westlich des wichtigsten Straßengebiets gelegenen Grund.
Das Ernährungsamtsgebiet von Udine ist mit der Stadt und dem lokalen wie regionalen Straßennetz bestens verbunden. Hier sind bereits die größten Niederlassungen, die auf dem Vertriebsgebiet arbeiten, vertreten, weshalb für die Tätigkeit der Farmaceutica Rinaldi die für ein bequemes Eintreffen der Lieferungen und ein effizientes, rasches Ausgabesystem an die Kundschaft wesentlichen Verbindungen gewährleistet sind. Der diese Tätigkeit aufnehmende neue Baukomplex entstand gänzlich unter Verwendung von Fertigteilträgerstrukturen, -abdeckungen und -ausfachungen aus Stahlbeton und besteht im wesentlichen aus drei Abschnitten mit spezifischer Bestimmung, welche in drei Teilen des anliegenden Gebäudes untergebracht, aber strukturell unterschiedlich sind.
- Die am östlichen Ende des Grunds befindlichen Büros verlaufen über zwei oberirdische Stockwerke in einem auf der Ostseite durch eine strukturelle Aluminiumfassade geschlossenen Flügel. Dieser ist teilweise transparent und mit Fensterflügeln aus Doppelkristall mit Glaskammerbildung zu öffnen und teilweise fest und blind mit aus MEG-Platten von Print bestehenden, isolierten Fensterflügeln. Letzteres Material verkleidet die Kopfteile des Büroflügels und einen Großteil der Südfassaden des Lagers, um mittels Bildung einer wärmeisolierten und belüfteten Fassade mäßigen Energieverbrauch und, in Zusammenhang mit der Bestimmung des Komplexes, hohen Schutz vor der sommerlichen Strahlung zu gewährleisten.
Unter den für die Büros bestimmten Stockwerken nimmt ein Untergeschoß das Archiv und die Anlagenzentralen auf.
- Der Mitarbeitereingang, die Umkleideräume und die Toiletten bilden die Verbindung zwischen dem Büroflügel und dem Lager. Diese Räume verlaufen auf einem einzigen Stockwerk, auch wenn auf einem Teil davon ein winziges Logis errichtet wurde, das für die Möglichkeit des Wachpersonals, sich auszuruhen, bestimmt ist.
- Der Hauptteil des Komplexes besteht aus dem Lager für Pharmamaterial und den für das Picking bestimmten automatisierten bzw. automatisierbaren Straßen, ist also für die Vorbereitung der für die verschiedenen Apotheken bestimmten Aufträge bestimmt. Das Lager bedient sich hingegen eines für die Ankunft der Lieferungen auf groß ausgelegten Lastkraftwagen bestimmten Sektors und eines weiteren für die Abfahrten, die mit Kleintransportern erfolgen, bestimmten.

Dieser Teil ist vor allem durch die Art gekennzeichnet, in welcher im Inneren das Picking und der mechanisierte Verschub der behandelten Artikel mittels modernster Anlagen erfolgen, die in direkter elektronischer Verbindung mit den Kundenfirmen äußerst komplexe Funktionen rasch durchführen können.
Von der Verkleidung dieses Gebäudeteils wird wegen der Rolle, die er spielt, ein hohes Leistungsniveau verlangt. Die MEG-Platten von Print, die neben den bereits beschriebenen Flügeln die Südfassade des Lagers verkleiden, übernehmen hier durch die Bildung einer belüfteten Wand eine wesentliche Rolle bei der Gewährleistung des Herabsetzung des sommerlichen Temperaturanstiegs. Die gleiche Maßnahme wurde für die Abdeckung getroffen, die durch Platten aus Zement, Luftkammer, wasserundurchlässigen Mantel und Wärmedämmschicht von großer Dicke an den flachen Teilen und durch wärmeisolierte Sandwichbauweise mäanderter Aluminiumplatten mit belüftetem Zwischenraum an den schrägen Teilen in Micro Shed-Ausbildung geschützt wird.
Zu diesen "passiven" Maßnahmen kommt eine starke High-Tech-Klimaanlage, die zusammen mit diesen die Erhaltung der für die Konservierung des Lagermaterials geeigneten Temperatur gewährleistet.
Zur Vervollständigung des Komplexes wurde in der Nähe des Fußgängereingangs zu den Büros die Trafo- und Abgabekabine von Enel errichtet, die dem Unternehmenspersonal direkt zugänglich ist.
Mit diesem kleinen Bau ist ein vertikales Element verbunden, das als Stütze für die Außenbeleuchtung der großen Plätze fungiert und in Form und Abmessungen das gleiche Element wiederholt, das auf der gegenüberliegenden Seite die Rauchkanäle aufnimmt.

Projekt:
Parmegiani Giacomuzzi Moore Associati
Ing. Giuliano Parmegiani, Arch. Lorenzo Giacomuzzi Moore.

Anlagenprojekt:
TE.S.I. srl
Tecnologie e Servizi per l'impiantistica.

Strukturberechnungen:
Ing. Antonio Battistella.

Durchführung:
Impresa Tobia Clocchiatti spa
Tesi System srl
Isalf
Conditerm srl
Claudio Tonutti - Impianti Elettrici.

Pab

Entwurf von Studio Kairos
B&B Italia

Pab stützt sich auf eine sehr einfache Idee: eine lange Platte, die zur Hälfte gebogen ist und von leichten Spannstangen gehalten wird, die wie Zeichen erscheinen. Das Ganze wird zu einer fortlaufenden Ablagefläche, die in der Länge und in der Höhe anpassungsfähig ist und bereits genügt, um auch sehr beschränkte Einrichtungsgegebenheiten zu bestimmen.

Andere Elemente wie Glaspaneelen, um Rauminhalte oder Oberflächen abzuschirmen, Behälter, um kleine Gegenstände abzulegen, robuste Bänke, denen dünne Konsolen entgegengesetzt sind, erlauben eine geometrische Gliederung des Systems sowohl bezüglich der Farbkombinationen als auch bezüglich der unterschiedlichen Ausmaße.

Die Konsole, Grundelement des Systems Pab, Ergebnis einer komplexen Projektsarbeit auf Materialien und Technologien, bringt Minimalismus, Einfachheit, Eleganz, Qualität der Details und Ökologie zum Ausdruck. Durch die Verwendung verschiedener Materialien wie Birkenholz oder Aluminium kann das System Pab in verschiedenen Habitats leben. Die Konsole kann als Endbearbeitung der Kopfstücke ein Eckelement aus Aluminium haben.

Pab, von deutlich funktionalistischer Auffassung, fügt zu den Konsolen Rückenlehnenelemente aus satiniert lackiertem Holz mit Stützfunktionen für die CD-Ablagen und Laden und Bänke aus Birkenholz mit Mehrzweckfunktionen hinzu, von der einfachen, weitläufigen Abstellfläche für Gegenstände zur TV- oder Hi-Fi-Stellage. Unter weiterer Berücksichtigung der Fähigkeit des Systems, auch den Lebensraum leben zu lassen und somit diskret aufzutreten, schälte sich das Behälterelement mit einer einfachen, aus einer säurebehandelten Kristalltür bestehenden Abschirmung heraus, die sich zwischen den Konsolen verschiebt und einen Rauminhalt mit der Möglichkeit der Ausstattung mit Kristallfächern oder Laden verbirgt. Die Behälter mit Klapptür oder Birkenholzladen schaffen mit den anderen Elementen des Systems ein konsequentes Verhältnis zeitgenössischer Ausdrucksweise, die in ästhetischer Einfachheit, praktischen Eigenschaften, Zugänglichkeit, aber auch mit einer präzisen Identität zusammengefaßt werden kann.

3D Bank
Ein System für die neuen Bankschalter
Castelli

Die Unternehmen, welche Büro- und Gemeinschaftseinrichtungen in ihrem Programm haben, müssen ihre Projekte unter Einbeziehung der verschiedenen ein Projekt bildenden Aspekte vorbereiten: Design, Innovation und Funktionalität. Letzere ist nichts anderes als die Resultante einer aus Ergonomie, Studium der neuen Technologien und sorgfältiger Analyse der Entwicklungen in der Arbeitswelt bestehenden Gleichung. Die Welt der Banken im besonderen hat wesentliche Änderungen erfahren, die auf die derzeitigen Ansprüche in der Geldgebarung zurückzuführen sind. Das Papiergeld verliert zum Vorteil der magnetischen Karten Punkte; die traditionelle Bankhinterlegung als Sparform wird durch Investitionsgebarung ersetzt. Die Bankstrategien müssen den Bedürfnissen eines in Entwicklung befindlichen Markts gegenüber, der an neuen Produkten und Leistungen interessiert ist, empfänglicher sein.

Daraus geht hervor, daß sich das Layout der Bankschalter radikal ändern und eine echte Revolution vornehmen muß, die nicht nur zur Ausrüstung mit den neuen Technologien, sondern auch zu einem Eingreifen der internen Bankorganisation führen wird.

Castelli antwortet auf die erneuerten Bedürfnisse mit 3D Bank, einem angesichts dieser Ideen entworfenen System. Neben der traditionellen Theke finden für die Beratung bestimmte Arbeitsplätze Raum, die vom Kunden leicht erkannt werden können, sowie Konferenzen vorbehaltene Sektoren und bequeme Wartebezirke. Bei Entwurf des Layout wird die Anordnung der Einrichtungen studiert, wobei von den strukturellen Beschränkungen ausgegangen wird, um einen idealen Pfad zu zeichnen, dank dessen der Kunde alle Servicestellen leicht erreichen kann, vom SB-Informatiksektor über den traditionellen Schalter zu der für die Beratung

bestimmten Zone.

Die Einfachheit der Zusammenstellung von 3D Bank ermöglicht so eine stark individuelle Gestaltung der Räume und leicht machbare Änderungen, ob diese nun auf die Bedürfnisse der Kundschaft oder auf die technologische Innovation zurückgehen, wodurch die beste Lösung erzielt wird. Auch vom formalen Standpunkt aus lassen die vielfachen Ausarbeitungen der Elemente dem Designer umfangreiche Möglichkeiten, sich sein eigenes Einrichtungssystem zu schaffen, da er von vielen Beschränkungen befreit ist.

Die Änderungen des Heims
Chiosco
Möbelserie von Luca Meda
Molteni & C.

Mode. Nun, im Namen der Liebe, die Du für die sieben Todsünden hast, bleib' doch manchmal stehen und sieh mich an.

Tod. Ich sehe Dich an.

Mode. Kennst Du mich nicht?

Tod. Du müßtest wissen, daß ich schlecht sehe und keine Brille tragen kann, weil die Engländer keine solchen machen, die dafür stünden, und wenn sie welche machten, hätte ich nichts, wo ich sie lafettieren könnte.

Mode. Ich bin die Mode, Deine Schwester.

Tod. Meine Schwester?

Mode. Ja, erinnerst Du Dich nicht daran, daß wir beide von der Vergänglichkeit geboren wurden?

Tod. Was soll ich mich erinnern, der ich der Erzfeind des Gedächtnisses bin!

Mode. Aber ich erinnere mich gut daran. Und ich weiß, daß wir beide gleichermaßen daran arbeiten, die Dinge von hier unten ständig zunichte zu machen und umzuändern, auch wenn Du zu diesem Zweck einen Weg einschlägst und ich einen anderen.

Tod. Falls Du nicht durch Deine Gedanken sprichst oder jemanden, den Du in der Gurgel hast, erhebe Deine Stimme mehr und sprich die Worte deutlicher aus. Wenn Du mit diesem Spinnwebstimmchen zwischen den Zähnen zu mir murmelst, verstehe ich Dich morgen, denn das Gehör, falls Du es nicht weißt, dient mir nicht besser als die Sehkraft.

Mode. Obwohl ich gegen die Gesittung bin und es in Frankreich nicht üblich ist, zu sprechen, um gehört zu werden, werde ich dennoch sprechen, wie Du es wünschst, weil wir Geschwister sind und uns untereinander ohne zuviel Respekt verhalten können. Ich sage, daß es unsere gemeinsame Natur und Brauch sind, die Welt ständig zu erneuern, doch warfst Du Dich von Anfang an auf die Menschen und das Blut. Ich gebe mich großteils mit den Bärten und Haartrachten, den Kleidern, dem Hausrat, den Palästen und dergleichen zufrieden. [...] Wenn wir ein Pferderennen zusammen zu bestreiten hätten, wüßte ich nicht, wer von uns beiden den Bewerb gewänne, denn Du läufst zwar, ich aber galoppiere am liebsten...

Die Mode galoppiert also enthemmt, mit unbeständigen, unerwarteten Schritten, wobei sie die Dinge ständig zunichte macht und verdreht. Giacomo Leopardi verschwägert sie in seiner *Operetta morale* mit Mutter Vergänglichkeit und Bruder Tod, wobei er von ihr als großer Macht spricht, die imstande ist, die stabilsten, ältesten Dinge anzugreifen. So bezieht sie auch "Hausrat" und "Paläste" mit ein, das Antlitz des Heims und die Nippessachen, die Möbel und die Formen. Und durch diese Einbeziehung schleppt sie sie in eine ewige, hinfällige Verfolgung von Angelegenheiten und Geschmäckern. Dies ist also der Punkt: wie sich das Heim dem Vorgehen, Fortschreiten und plötzlichem Wenden des Lebens anpassen kann, ohne deshalb in die Untugenden der Mode, in ihre Vergänglichkeit, in ihr äußeres Spiel des Scheins zu stürzen.

Und der Beginn einer Antwort kann vielleicht aus dieser Entscheidung kommen: Die Möbel in die Lage zu versetzen, ihre Aufstellung und ihr Bild innerhalb gewisser Grenzen zu ändern, und zwar im Laufe des Tages ebenso wie im weitläufigeren Raum ihrer Existenz, ausgehend von ihrer "theatralischen" Natur. Diese Theatralik entspringt einem ihnen innewohnenden Charakter, weshalb sie als Kulisse und Hintergrund auftreten, denn sie bilden die häusliche "Bühne", den für die Aufnahme der wandelbaren Angelegenheiten des täglichen Lebens bestimmten Rahmen. Diese mögliche "Kunst", die Möbel den Umständen "anzupassen", betrifft die Anordnung in den Zimmern ebenso wie die gegenseitigen Überlagerungen, die Fähigkeit zur Aufnahme von Personen und Gesten, die Anpassungsfähigkeit bei der Reaktion auf Ereignisse und Bedürfnisse. Eine durch die neuen technischen Möglichkeiten, das fortgeschrittene Niveau der Technologien, welche die Möbel schließlich verkörpern, machbar gewordene "Kunst". Sigfried Giedion, der größte Erzähler der Modernität, sah die Zukunft des Heims in dem Sinne, daß "mechanisation takes command", "die Mechanisierung das Kommando übernimmt", wie der Titel seines berühmten Buches lautete. Heute glauben wir nicht an diesen allgemeinen Mythos, sondern an ein neues, subtileres, von den Materialien, Vorrichtungen, Bewegungen und Kombinationen garantiertes System der Möglichkeiten. Eine Anpassungsfähigkeit, die die formale Stabilität und die Tradition des Heims nicht verraten soll.

Daniele Vitale

Chiosco

"Ich möchte einen roten Kiosk mit vergoldeten Minaretten, / mit dünnen Alabastersäulen..." (Théophile Gautier)
Chiosco ist eine Reihe koordinierter Möbel, die für die Bereiche des Heims mit öffentlichem und repräsentativem Charakter entworfen wurden. Sie besteht in erster Linie aus Möbeln, die als Schaufenster und Behälter gedacht sind. Sie sind geschlossen oder halbverschlossen verglast und mit der Typologie von Kredenzen oder Bücherschränken, Backtrögen oder Vitrinen verwandt. Neben ihnen bestehen aber auch "Tagesstrukturen", an die Wände gehängte und von dünnen Einschnitten durchfurchte Holzprospekte, die Regale und Laden ohne sichtbare Stütze und ohne Zugstangen zu tragen vermögen. Die Regale können sich in scharnierversehene, je nach den Bedürfnissen und Momenten einmal offene, einmal geschlossene "Klappen" verwandeln, also ihre Dienste anbieten oder sich zurückhaltend schließen und der Wand angleichen. "Prospekte", die mit Leichtigkeit stützen, aber auch als kleine "Theaterszenerie" auftreten, die die vor sie gesetzten Dinge hervorhebt. Im besonderen können niedrige Möbel und Bänke, die Fernsehgerät und Radioapparat, Computer und Hi-Fi-Anlage auf rationelle Weise aufnehmen, davor gestellt werden. Aber die Serie umfaßt auch ergänzende Möbel wie Eßtische und -stühle, Schreibtische, kleine Kommoden, Uhren, Konsolen, Beistell- und Dekorationstischchen, kleine, unabhängige Möbel zum Schützen und Vorzeigen von Gegenständen: viele verschiedene Stücke, die einen allgemeinen Vorschlag für das Heim aufzubauen verstehen. Chiosco basiert auf dem formalen Prinzip der Unterscheidung des Interieurs vom Exterieur und der vertikalen Strukturen von den horizontalen Fächern. Die vertikalen Strukturen sind aus Birnenholz, die Fächer mit einem zart elfenbeinfarbenen Lack gestrichen. Chiosco spielt also auf harmonischen Beziehungen zwischen naturbelassenen Materialien und Glanz der Verkleidungen. Chiosco bedient sich technisch hochraffinierter Elemente und Teile. Die für die Bewegung bestimmten Vorrichtungen wie Scharniere, Kufen, Kolben, Fahrgestelle werden verkleinert und verborgen; aus ihnen werden kleine, kostbare Objekte, die einmal eingefaßt, ein andermal verborgen werden. Und den Bewegungen wird die Strenge geometrischer Genauigkeiten verliehen.